Global Leadership
Case Studies of Business Leaders in Japan
Yasuo Nakatani   Ryan Smithers

KINSEIDO

Kinseido Publishing Co., Ltd.
3-21 Kanda Jimbo-cho, Chiyoda-ku,
Tokyo 101-0051, Japan

Copyright © 2015 by Yasuo Nakatani
　　　　　　　　　　 Ryan Smithers

All rights reserved. No part of this publication may be reproduced, stored in a retrieval system, or transmitted, in any form or by any means, electronic, mechanical, photocopying, recording or otherwise, without the prior permission of the publisher.

First published 2015 by Kinseido Publishing Co., Ltd.

Cover design　　Takayuki Minegishi
Text design　　　P & A

音声ファイル無料ダウンロード

http://www.kinsei-do.co.jp/download/4001

この教科書で DL 00 の表示がある箇所の音声は、上記 URL または QR コードにて無料でダウンロードできます。自習用音声としてご活用ください。

- ▶ PC からのダウンロードをお勧めします。スマートフォンなどでダウンロードされる場合は、ダウンロード前に「解凍アプリ」をインストールしてください。
- ▶ URL は、検索ボックスではなくアドレスバー (URL 表示欄) に入力してください。
- ▶ お使いのネットワーク環境によっては、ダウンロードできない場合があります。

CD 00　左記の表示がある箇所の音声は、教室用 CD（Class Audio CD）に収録されています。

はじめに

□臨場感あふれるビジネスケースでリーダーシップを学ぶ

　グローバルリーダーになるためには、どのような条件が必要なのだろうか。本書は日本の代表的な企業における実際の15のビジネスケースを取り扱い、国際社会で活躍をめざす人のロールモデルを示している。英語学習を通して、リーダーシップとは何か、それをどのように身に付け、いかに発揮すべきかを実例で学んでいく。

　全ての章の内容は、筆者が直接インタビューを行い作成したケーススタディに基づいている。このため、単なる企業の歴史や概要ではなく、グローバル化が進む中で、実際に起こった困難なミッションに対して、当事者が必死になってリーダーシップを発揮した臨場感あふれる内容となっている。

□もしあなたがリーダーなら、次のようなグローバルな課題をどう解決するか？

- 世界最大の共同＝協働マーケティング "Intel Inside" の基本のモデルは、なぜ日本から始める必要があったのか？

- 日本コカ・コーラは、どうやって消費者が環境保護活動に参加するように促したのだろう？

- 当初、日本であまり成功しなかったシャネルやディオールをどうすれば強いブランドに育てられるのか？

- 順調に成長していた無印良品を展開する良品計画は、業績が急に低迷し、海外の店舗も閉じなければならなかった。何が原因で、どう解決すべきなのか？

- 資生堂がイタリアや中国でナンバーワンのブランドになるには、どのようなマーケティング戦略が必要なのか？

- 東芝のテレビを売るために、たった独りで人脈も販売ルートもない未開発のベトナムを訪ねた時、いったい何から始めればよいのか。また、同社はビジネスの急激なグローバル化に対応するため、20万人近くもいるグループ社員に対して、どのような人材開発をすべきだろう？

- 高速船ジェットフォイルで福岡・釜山航路に参入したJR九州は、韓国企業の市場参入のため利益が激減してしまった。強力なライバルにどのように対処するのか？

　本書では、その他いくつかのケースを英語で学び、自分はどのようにリーダーシップを発揮すべきなのか考えていく。リーダーに必要な決断力や、コミットメントの方法を疑似体験しながら身に付けることができる。

□**ビジネスや経営の基礎知識を英語で楽しく学ぶ**
　一見難しそうなマーケティングや経営戦略に関する英語のビジネス語句およびコンセプトを、実際にあったおもしろいケースで学ぶことで自然に理解ができるようになる。

□**英語の内容理解をTOEIC形式に準じた問題で確認できる**
　TOEICテストで高得点をめざすには、ビジネスの基礎知識も必要である。本書の問題演習の中には、TOEICの出題形式に準じているものもある。グローバルに活躍するリーダーに関する重要な事象を扱ったケースを通して学んだビジネス英語の成果を各章で確認できる。

　グローバル人材の育成が叫ばれる昨今、ビジネス界における真のグローバルリーダーの姿を英語で学び、その体験を通して、今度は読者のみなさんが新たなグローバル人材として世界に羽ばたく一助に本書がなれば幸いと考える。

　　　　　　　　　　　　　　　　　　　　　　　　　　　　　　　　　著者

本書の構成と効果的な使い方

▶ **Mission!**
- 各ケースで取り上げたビジネスケースの背景知識を日本語で理解し、英語学習の準備をする。リーダーが解決しなければならない問題を提示している。

▶ **Vocabulary — Bottom-up Activity**
- 本文理解に役立つビジネス英語を中心とした重要語句を意味選択の問題演習で確認する。
- CD の音声を聞き、発音練習をして重要語句の意識化を図る。

▶ **Listening — Scanning Activity**
- 上で学んだ重要語句を中心に単語のディクテーションをする。
- TOEIC テスト Part 4 形式に類似した問題で、リスニングにより内容理解を確認する。

▶ **Reading**
- 上記の Activity によりリーディングの準備ができた上で長文の読解を行う。
- TOEIC テスト Part 7 形式に類似した長文問題で内容理解を深める。
- CD の音声を聞き、内容理解を確認する。

▶ **Notes**
- ビジネス知識のあまりない学習者は、事前に少し難度の高い語句を日本語で確認しておく。

▶ **Business Focus**
- ケースを理解するのに必要な語句などの説明をもとに、現代ビジネスで重要なマーケティングや戦略、交渉術などの基本的な事例を学ぶ。

▶ **Tasks for Global Leadership**

Task 1　Discuss the Points
- 各ビジネスケースの重要点を要約した対話文を通して、内容の再確認とディクテーションの練習を行う。

Task 2　Write Down the Points
- 各章の重要な語句やビジネス関連の語句を再確認し、正確に書けるようにする。

■ 本書は CheckLink (チェックリンク) 対応テキストです。

CheckLinkのアイコンが表示されている設問は、CheckLinkに対応しています。
CheckLinkを使用しなくても従来通りの授業ができますが、特色をご理解いただき、授業活性化のためにぜひご活用ください。

CheckLinkの特色について

　大掛かりで複雑な従来のe-learningシステムとは異なり、CheckLinkのシステムは大きな特色として次の3点が挙げられます。

1. これまで行われてきた教科書を使った授業展開に大幅な変化を加えることなく、専門的な知識なしにデジタル学習環境を導入することができる。
2. PC教室やCALL教室といった最新の機器が導入された教室に限定されることなく、普通教室を使用した授業でもデジタル学習環境を導入することができる。
3. 授業中での使用に特化し、教師・学習者双方のモチベーション・集中力をアップさせ、授業自体を活性化することができる。

▶教科書を使用した授業に「デジタル学習環境」を導入できる

　本システムでは、学習者は教科書のCheckLinkのアイコンが表示されている設問にPCやスマートフォン、携帯電話端末からインターネットを通して解答します。そして教師は、授業中にリアルタイムで解答結果を把握し、正解率などに応じて有効な解説を行うことができるようになっています。教科書自体は従来と何ら変わりはありません。解答の手段としてCheckLinkを使用しない場合でも、従来通りの教科書として使用して授業を行うことも、もちろん可能です。

▶教室環境を選ばない

　従来の多機能なe-learning教材のように学習者側の画面に多くの機能を持たせることはせず、「解答する」ことに機能を特化しました。PCだけでなく、一部タブレット端末やスマートフォン、携帯電話端末からの解答も可能です。したがって、PC教室やCALL教室といった大掛かりな教室は必要としません。普通教室でもCheckLinkを用いた授業が可能です。教師はPCだけでなく、一部タブレット端末やスマートフォンからも解答結果の確認をすることができます。

▶授業を活性化するための支援システム

　本システムは予習や復習のツールとしてではなく、授業中に活用されることで真価を発揮する仕組みになっています。CheckLinkというデジタル学習環境を通じ、教師と学習者双方が授業中に解答状況などの様々な情報を共有することで、学習者はやる気を持って解答し、教師は解答状況に応じて効果的な解説を行う、という好循環を生み出します。CheckLinkは、普段の授業をより活力のあるものへと変えていきます。

　上記3つの大きな特色以外にも、掲示板などの授業中に活用できる機能を用意しています。従来通りの教科書としても使用はできますが、ぜひCheckLinkの機能をご理解いただき、普段の授業をより活性化されたものにしていくためにご活用ください。

CheckLink の使い方

CheckLinkは、PCや一部タブレット端末、スマートフォン、携帯電話端末を用いて、この教科書の CheckLink のアイコン表示のある設問に解答するシステムです。
- 初めて CheckLink を使う場合、以下の要領で**「学習者登録」**と**「教科書登録」**を行います。
- 一度登録を済ませれば、あとは毎回**「ログイン画面」**から入るだけです。CheckLinkを使う教科書が増えたときだけ、改めて**「教科書登録」**を行ってください。

CheckLink URL

https://checklink.kinsei-do.co.jp/student/

QRコードの読み取りができる端末の場合はこちらから ▶▶▶

ご注意ください！ 上記URLは**「検索ボックス」**でなく**「アドレスバー(URL表示欄)」**に入力してください。

▶学習者登録

① 上記URLにアクセスすると、右のページが表示されます。学校名を入力し「ログイン画面へ」をクリックしてください。
PCの場合は「PC用はこちら」をクリックして PC用ページを表示します。同様に学校名を入力し「ログイン画面へ」をクリックしてください。

② ログイン画面が表示されたら**「初めての方はこちら」**をクリックし「学習者登録画面」に入ります。

③ 自分の学籍番号、氏名、メールアドレス(学校のメールなど**PCメールを推奨**)を入力し、次に**任意のパスワード**を8桁以上20桁未満(半角英数字)で入力します。なお、学籍番号はパスワードとして使用することはできません。

④ 「パスワード確認」は、❸で入力したパスワードと同じものを入力します。

⑤ 最後に「登録」ボタンをクリックして登録は完了です。次回からは、「ログイン画面」から学籍番号とパスワードを入力してログインしてください。

▶教科書登録

①ログイン後、メニュー画面から「教科書登録」を選び（PCの場合はその後「新規登録」ボタンをクリック）、「教科書登録」画面を開きます。

②教科書と受講する授業を登録します。
教科書の最終ページにある、**教科書固有番号**のシールをはがし、印字された**16桁の数字とアルファベット**を入力します。

③授業を担当される先生から連絡された**11桁の授業ID**を入力します。

④最後に「登録」ボタンをクリックして登録は完了です。

⑤実際に使用する際は「教科書一覧」（PCの場合は「教科書選択画面」）の該当する教科書名をクリックすると、「問題解答」の画面が表示されます。

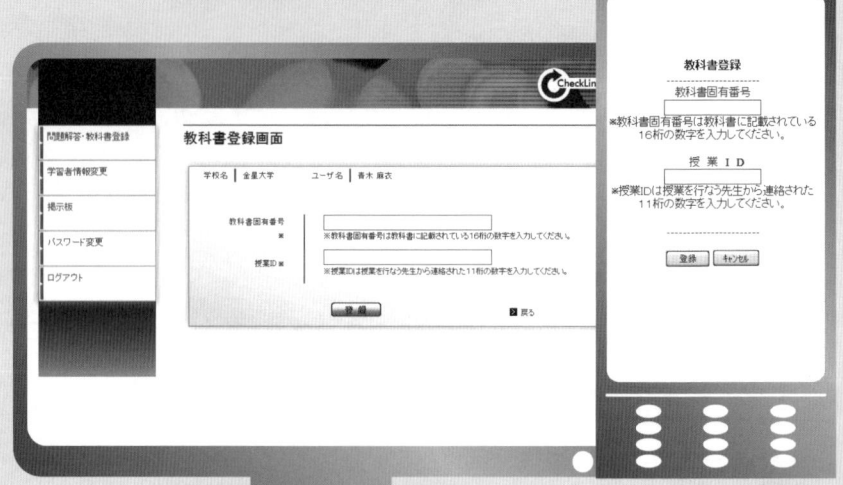

▶問題解答

①問題は教科書を見ながら解答します。この教科書の CheckLink のアイコン表示のある設問に解答できます。

②問題が表示されたら選択肢を選びます。

③表示されている問題に解答した後、「解答」ボタンをクリックすると解答が登録されます。

▶CheckLink 推奨環境

PC

推奨 OS
- Windows XP, Vista 以降
- Macintosh OS X 以降
- Linux

推奨ブラウザ
- Internet Explorer 6.0 以上
- Firefox 3.0 以上
- Safari
- Opera
- Google Chrome

携帯電話・スマートフォン
- 3G 以降の携帯電話（docomo, au, softbank）
- iPhone, iPad
- Android OS スマートフォン、タブレット

▶CheckLink 開発

CheckLink は奥田裕司 福岡大学教授、正興 IT ソリューション株式会社、株式会社金星堂によって共同開発されました。

CheckLink は株式会社金星堂の登録商標です。

CheckLink の使い方に関するお問い合わせは…

正興 IT ソリューション株式会社　CheckLink 係

e-mail　checklink@seiko-denki.co.jp

Contents

はじめに
本書の構成と効果的な使い方
CheckLink について

Act 1　Global Marketing　グローバル・マーケティング

Case 1　Initiating World's Biggest Joint Marketing Project ……………………… 2
世界最大の共同＝協働マーケティングを立ち上げる ── インテル株式会社

Case 2　Creating Value and Making a Difference ……………………………… 8
新しい価値を創造し変化をもたらす ── 日本コカ・コーラ株式会社

Case 3　Enhancing Luxury Brand Identity …………………………………… 14
日本の消費者に向けたブランド構築
　　── シャネル株式会社、パルファン・クリスチャン・ディオール・ジャポン株式会社

Act 2　Business Strategies　ビジネス・ストラテジー

Case 4　Changing a Big Company with Management of Technology ………… 20
技術経営で大企業に変革を起こす ── サッポロビール株式会社

Case 5　Reviving a Leading Brand ……………………………………………… 26
時代をリードするブランドの再生 ── 株式会社良品計画

Case 6　Negotiating with Headquarters ……………………………………… 32
アメリカ本社との交渉戦術で日本の品質管理を世界標準に ── インテル株式会社

Case 7　Making a Challenging Business Profitable ………………………… 38
困難なビジネスを長期的展望で黒字化に ── JR九州高速船株式会社

Contents

Act 3 Localization　ローカリゼーション

Case 8 Becoming a Representative Corporate Citizen in China …………… 44
中国人のためのブランド作りと企業活動 ── 株式会社資生堂

Case 9 Developing New Business in Emerging Markets ……………………… 50
新興国の開拓者 ── 株式会社東芝

Case 10 De-centralizing Marketing Strategies …………………………………… 56
日本の消費者に伝わるコミュニケーション戦略 ── インテル株式会社

Case 11 Competing with Big Companies by Establishing a Regional Brand …… 62
地域密着ブランドで全国ブランドに対抗する ── 株式会社明月堂

Act 4 Globalization　グローバリゼーション

Case 12 Sustaining Brand Identity and Global Business Strategies …………… 68
ブランド・アイデンティティの持続とグローバルビジネス戦略 ── 株式会社良品計画

Case 13 Enhancing Global Brand Communication ……………………………… 74
グローバルブランドコミュニケーションの向上 ── 株式会社資生堂

Case 14 Developing a Global Leader for Diversity Management ……………… 80
グローバルリーダーの育成をめざすダイバーシティ経営 ── 株式会社東芝

Case 15 Building Global Business Models ………………………………………… 86
グローバルビジネスモデルの構築 ── コニカミノルタ株式会社

謝辞

Case 1

Act 1　Global Marketing

Initiating World's Biggest Joint Marketing Project

世界最大の共同＝協働マーケティングを立ち上げる

インテル株式会社

Mission!　企業の知名度を上げろ！

　インテルの日本法人は半導体製品で確固たる信頼を得ていたが、顧客の中心はパソコン製造業者が占めるいわゆる「B2Bビジネス」で、一般の消費者には企業としてのブランドが確立されていなかった。特に、日本の大学生は就職先としてテレビコマーシャルなどを多く放映している大手企業を好む傾向があった。また、外資系の企業は簡単に人員を削減するというネガティブなイメージもあったことから、優秀な人材の採用は容易でなかった。このような状況を改善するため、当時の日本法人で取締役副社長を務めていた傳田にとって、いかに一般消費者に向けたブランド構築を行えばよいのかが大きな課題であった。

Vocabulary — Bottom-up Activity

CheckLink　DL 02　CD1-02

次の英語に合う日本語を選び記号で答えなさい。

1. marketer　　　　　　（　）　　(A) 解雇する
2. semiconductor　　　（　）　　(B) マーケティングを実施する人
3. general consumer　（　）　　(C) 本社
4. lay off　　　　　　　（　）　　(D) 一般消費者
5. resistance　　　　　（　）　　(E) 反対、反抗
6. reliability　　　　　（　）　　(F) 信頼性
7. headquarters　　　（　）　　(G) 半導体

Listening — Scanning Activity

音声を聞いて空所を埋めなさい。

It has been argued that the "Intel Inside" program has become the most successful cooperative marketing strategy in the world since its ¹_____ in 1991. However, it is not very well known that this strategy began in Japan in 1989. The CEO of Intel Japan and an outstanding marketer from Dentsu Inc. made things happen by attempting to improve the brand image of Intel in Japan. Although Intel had ²_____ its position as a leading semiconductor company in many countries around the world, it was not well known by general consumers in Japan. Intel was mainly involved in B2B sales, with their operations centered on computer manufacturers. As a result, the company did not have to advertise on TV or through other mediums. Unfortunately though, this unfamiliarity with the Intel brand among ³_____ consumers affected Intel Japan's recruiting activities negatively. That is to say, talented Japanese university students ⁴_____ to pursue jobs at large well-known companies.

NOTES
cooperative 共同の　marketing strategy マーケティング戦略　outstanding 際立った
make things happen 事を起こす　B2B 企業同士の取引（Business to Business の略）
manufacturer 製造業者、メーカー　medium 媒体　That is to say つまり

設問を聞いて最も適切な選択肢を選びなさい。

1. Who was instrumental in helping improve Intel Japan's image?
   (A) A TV advertising representative
   (B) A salesman from Dentsu
   (C) An Internet authority
   (D) The CEO of a major computer manufacturing company

2. Why did Intel suffer from brand recognition problems in Japan?
   (A) Because they did not advertise effectively.
   (B) Because they were not popular with university students.
   (C) Because they did not recruit aggressively enough.
   (D) Because the company had a bad reputation.

Reading

以下の英文を読み、質問の答えとして最も適切な選択肢を選びなさい。

Improving Brand Recognition

Denda, who was a manager at Intel Japan, tried to recruit promising new university graduates in order to expand the business, but the parents of prospective new recruits, particularly mothers, preferred their children to work at famous Japanese companies that advertised on TV frequently. Also, Japanese parents had a negative image toward foreign capital companies that typically do not think twice when it comes to laying off employees that have become redundant or ineffective. Accordingly, Japanese students influenced by their parents' opinions tended not to give much consideration to working at Intel. Denda needed to change the bad impressions that many Japanese had about the company, but going about this was not an easy task since their main customers were computer manufacturers and there was no need for Intel to advertise their products on TV.

Eventually when Intel Japan decided to consult with a major advertising agency, Dentsu Inc., only a few of their marketers could appreciate the value of computer engineering. As a result, the company assigned the project to Kamo because of his experience in working on Microsoft's initial advertising campaign. When Kamo met to discuss his idea with Denda, Denda realized that the project's potential was great, but the main problem was how to bring recognition to a product that functioned out of sight of the consumer. That is, the significant roles that Intel CPUs (Central Processing Unit) play inside of computers needed to be recognized by end-consumers. After much contemplation Kamo realized that Dolby noise reduction systems installed in music players operate on principles similar to Intel's. People cannot see Dolby's proprietary technology, but they can see Dolby's trademark symbol on many high-quality audio products. Accordingly, he came up with the idea to put Intel stickers on computers to let consumers notice that its CPU was inside. When the clients agreed to join this campaign, Intel agreed to compensate them according to the number of stickers they utilized. This project was named "Intel in it."

1. Why did Intel Japan struggle to recruit new university graduates?
    (A) Because marketers could not understand the value of computer engineering.
    (B) Because Intel CPUs did not perform significantly.
    (C) Because Intel did not actively recruit at Japanese universities.
    (D) Because parents feared foreign companies.

2. How did Intel Japan solve their image problem?
   (A) They hired Denda.
   (B) They advertised on TV.
   (C) They imitated Microsoft's initial advertising campaign.
   (D) They advertised on computers.

"Intel in it"

When Kamo proposed the project idea to Denda, he was immediately convinced of its potential success. Unfortunately, the idea faced some initial resistance from companies that were against double branding. Large Japanese computer manufactures, such as Fujitsu and NEC, had already established a strong brand image and they did not feel that they needed the support of suppliers, like Intel, to better guarantee product reliability. Moreover, the top executives of these companies did not want to see another company's logo on their products. At that time though, Toshiba was attempting to develop the first notebook-type computer in the world, and they needed a new and smaller CPU that would produce less heat. Intel could develop a CPU with their advanced technology to meet Toshiba's specifications, but the price was going to be higher than what Toshiba was willing to pay.

Denda negotiated with Mizoguchi who was the PC division director at Toshiba. He promised Mizoguchi that if the company agreed to join the "Intel in it" campaign, he would persuade Intel headquarters to develop the CPU that Toshiba needed at a reasonable price, so that Toshiba could continue to keep their products priced to sell in large quantities. After pondering the offer the director said yes without even getting the go-ahead from the top executives of Toshiba because he believed they would resist the proposal of double branding. After getting the go-ahead from Mizoguchi, Denda successfully convinced Intel headquarters to produce a special CPU for Toshiba by explaining the great potential of the notebook computer market. In 1989, Toshiba launched their first notebook computer called "Dynabook" and on all of the laptops were official stickers that said "Intel in it." The result of this double branding created unprecedented success for both companies. Shortly afterwards Intel headquarters realized the value of the campaign and expanded the campaign worldwide in 1991 with a new sticker, "Intel Inside." This global joint marketing strategy went on to propel Intel's brand value to third in the world.

3. How did Mizoguchi get approval from top executives for double branding?
 (A) He simply explained the merits of the plan.
 (B) He got Intel to develop a new CPU.
 (C) He explained the potential of laptop computers to the board.
 (D) He didn't get approval.

4. What slogan made Intel famous the world over?
 (A) Dynabook
 (B) Intel Inside
 (C) Intel in it
 (D) Intel

NOTES

foreign capital company 外資系企業　think twice 熟考する
when it comes to... …のことになると　redundant 余剰な　give consideration to... …を考慮する
go about... …にとりかかる　out of sight of... …の見えないところで
CPU (Central Processing Unit) 中央演算処理装置　end-consumer（店頭などで購入する）最終消費者
proprietary technology 専有技術

---

supplier 納入業者　specification 仕様（スペック）　get the go-ahead 承認を得る
unprecedented 前例のない　propel 押し上げる

Business Focus

- **cooperative marketing**　共同＝協働マーケティング
  企業間で協力して広告活動などを行うこと。おたがいのブランドを補完したり、共同のイベントやキャンペーンを行ったりする場合などに活用される。

- **B2B (Business to Business)**　企業同士の取引
  製造業者などへ原材料や部品を販売するビジネスのこと。完成品などを消費者に直接販売するB2C (Business to Consumer) とは異なり、広告宣伝をあまり必要としない。

- **double branding**　ダブルブランド
  たとえばインテルは、製品の購入業者がテレビや新聞・雑誌などに広告を出す際にインテルのロゴマークや宣伝を入れると、購入額に応じ広告費用の一部をサポートした。これによって、有名でない企業がパソコンを販売する際は品質を保証するものにもなる。

Tasks for Global Leadership

Task 1 Discuss the Points

DL 07   CD1-07

本ケースのポイントに関する次の会話を聞いて、空所を埋めなさい。

Mai: In this case, the main problem for Intel was how to bring recognition to the name of Intel because their product functioned out of sight of the consumer.

Bob: Based on that fact, Intel Japan requested an advertising agency come up with an idea for a new Intel logo, in which stickers were put on every PC to let consumers recognize that Intel's CPU was inside. This is how the world's biggest **1**_____ started.

Mai: Yes, but the campaign was not launched so easily. It **2**_____ from customers because of **3**_____.

Bob: Fortunately, Toshiba had been developing the world's first laptop computer at that time, so it was a chance for Intel to provide Toshiba with a new CPU targeted for the mobile PC market. This was the breakthrough they were looking for.

Mai: Hmm, yes. And although price was a problem, Denda promised Toshiba that he would **4**_____ their price if Toshiba agreed to join the campaign in Japan first. I think these actions demonstrate how to be a global leader.

Bob: You're right! Thus, in the business world when things seem fixed, it is great leaders that know **5**_____ by turning convention upside down to achieve something for the greatest good of a company. That's the point of this case.

Task 2 Write Down the Points

企業の知名度を上げるために、どのような行動が取られたか、本文および上の会話を参考にして、与えられた文字に続くように空所を埋めなさい。

1. Intel Japan **l**_____ an effective **m**_____ **c**_____ to bring recognition to their products.
2. Intel Japan could take advantage of **d**_____ **b**_____ when Toshiba needed a new CPU. That was the **b**_____ for them.
3. Denda promised Toshiba that he would **p**_____ **h**_____ to lower the price if Toshiba **a**_____ to **j**_____ the campaign.

Case 2

Act 1　Global Marketing

Creating Value and Making a Difference
新しい価値を創造し変化をもたらす

日本コカ・コーラ株式会社

Mission!　消費者に新しい価値を提供しよう！

　ザ コカ・コーラ カンパニーは1892年の設立以来、様々なマーケティング手法を創造し、消費者の支持を得て、今や同社の製品は1日に世界で18億杯も飲まれている。特に1923年からCEOを務めたRobert W. Woodruffは、企業のミッションを明確にして様々な改革を行い、同社を世界企業へと成長させた。日本コカ・コーラは1957年からビジネスを始め、自動販売機の技術開発や、新しい清涼飲料の開発などを通して世界的にリーダーシップを取ってきた。また、環境問題などにも配慮しながら、人々に感動や共感を与える新たな価値の創造にも取り組んできた。

Vocabulary — Bottom-up Activity

CheckLink　　DL 08　　CD1-08

次の英語に合う日本語を選び記号で答えなさい。

1. invent　　　　　　　　　　（　　）　　(A) ひねってつぶす
2. red barrel　　　　　　　　（　　）　　(B) 環境にやさしい
3. franchise structure　　　　（　　）　　(C) 赤い樽
4. driving force　　　　　　　（　　）　　(D) 発明する
5. vending machine　　　　　（　　）　　(E) 自動販売機
6. eco-friendly　　　　　　　（　　）　　(F) 促進する力
7. twisted and crushed　　　　（　　）　　(G) フランチャイズ方式

Listening — Scanning Activity

音声を聞いて空所を埋めなさい。

   The Coca-Cola Company is the biggest beverage producer in the world and operates businesses in more than 200 countries. The brand has been recognized as one of the world's leading brands, with sales of the company's products totaling more than 1.8 billion drinks a day. When pharmacist John Pemberton **1**_____ Coca-Cola in 1886, however, he only sold nine drinks a day. In 1892, Asa Candler took over the business from Pemberton and founded the Coca-Cola Company. With Candler at the helm, the company transported **2**_____ barrels of the company's syrup to shops where soda fountains were used to mix carbonated water with the syrup. The business developed well, but sales of the drink were significantly increased after two young lawyers got a contract to sell Coca-Cola in **3**_____ in 1899. This was the beginning of the Coca-Cola **4**_____ structure that spread out all over the world. In 1923, Robert W. Woodruff became the President of the Coca-Cola Company and led the company with excellent marketing strategies for decades, expanding the business internationally in 44 countries by the late 1930s.

NOTES
beverage 飲料　pharmacist 薬剤師　take over 引き継ぐ　at the helm 指揮を取って
soda fountain 清涼飲料水を店頭で提供する装置　carbonated water 炭酸水　decade 10年間

設問を聞いて最も適切な選択肢を選びなさい。

1. Coca-Cola was first sold in bottles by
    (A) two young lawyers
    (B) John Pemberton
    (C) Robert W. Woodruff
    (D) Asa Candler

2. According to the passage, when was Coca-Cola's influence abroad the greatest?
    (A) 1886　　(B) 1892　　(C) 1923　　(D) The late 1930s

Reading

以下の英文を読み、質問の答えとして最も適切な選択肢を選びなさい。

The Renown of Coca-Cola

It was Robert W. Woodruff who inspired not only the global nature of Coca-Cola, but also the company's current mission: to refresh the world, to inspire moments of optimism and happiness, and to create value and make a difference. These statements are the driving force behind the company's actions and act as a standard by which the company conducts business. In pursuit of its mission statement, Coca-Cola has accomplished several outstanding feats in marketing. For example, the company has been a sponsor of the Olympic Games since the Amsterdam Olympics in 1928, making it the longest-standing sponsor. The current popular image of a jolly Santa Claus in a red suit with a white beard was the creation of a Coca-Cola advertising campaign in 1931. During World War II, Woodruff responded to a request from the U.S. government to have Coca-Cola made available to U.S. soldiers around the world, and pledged that it would do so for five cents a bottle regardless of what it cost the Company to produce. All these exploits contributed greatly to the establishment of Coca-Cola as a prestigious brand, and although these deeds are credited to Woodruff, he acknowledged that "there is no limit to what a man can do or where he can go if he doesn't mind who gets the credit."

In 2009, the company set up their 2020 Vision with a goal of doubling the company's global business. They decided to take on individual strategies according to their three different target markets: the emerging market, the developing market, and the developed market. In a developed market such as Japan, they aim at driving profitable growth through innovation and productivity. In this regard, the Japanese Coca-Cola system, which consists of Coca-Cola Co, (Japan) Ltd. and eight local bottling partners, is expected to lead the company in the development of future growth for this market segment. Since the Coca-Cola Company penetrated the Japanese market in 1957, Japan has taken a leadership role among world operations in terms of innovating vending machines and developing new drinking products.

1. What did Coca-Cola NOT do to develop their brand image?
  (A) They supported the 1928 Olympics in Amsterdam.

(B) They made Coca-Cola available for five cents to U.S. soldiers around the world during World War II.
(C) They popularized Santa Claus.
(D) They established distribution centers in all battle zones.

2. How will Japan help promote future growth for the Coca-Cola Company?
(A) By helping develop the emerging market
(B) By contributing funds to developing markets
(C) By campaigning for future growth
(D) By creating new drinks

The Coca-Cola System in Japan   CheckLink   DL 12   CD1-12

In Japan, where vending machines dispense just about anything, Coca-Cola's market share of the 5.52 million vending machine market totals around one million machines. Accordingly, Coca-Cola has been working hard to be at the forefront of this market by innovating many new technologies such as hot and cold vending machines and cashless payment systems. Most recently they have introduced eco-friendly vending machines that eliminate green-house gases and minimize the use of electricity.

On top of Coca-Cola's innovative triumphs, the company has created such famous drinks as *Georgia Coffee, Aquarius and Ayataka*, to name a few. In fact, Coca-Cola Japan invented four of the 16 representative global brands with combined sales totaling more than one billion U.S. dollars annually. The success of these brands is linked to robust marketing campaigns and the sales efforts of the bottlers. In addition, the company pays careful attention to consumers' changing needs, so that their products reflect current trends in what and how drinks are drunk.

One example of Coca-Cola Japan's cutting-edge marketing success is "I LOHAS." Until recently, mainly imported mineral water products were sold in Japan, with most of the imported products utilizing blue bottles and labels to symbolize fresh water, while advertising focused on connecting the products to beautiful scenes of nature. I LOHAS on the other hand took a very different approach. This brand focused on the eco-friendliness of the product because of a survey that pointed out that while many Japanese understand the importance of being eco-friendly, they do not have any clear ideas on what to do. Thus, company engineers invented a thin plastic material that is 40 percent lighter than conventional PET bottles, so that empty I LOHAS bottles can be easily twisted and crushed to a smaller size. This means that every time someone buys I LOHAS water rather than another competing product, they are aiding the environment because the empty bottle reduces the amount of space and cost needed for recycling. In line with the eco-friendly nature of this product, green is used for the cap and design, while TV commercials have a famous actor demonstrate the ease with which the bottles are crushed. Customers are thereby encouraged to buy I LOHAS and become eco-friendly. This eco-friendly campaign has brought great success to I LOHAS, with over two billion bottles shipped during the first 3.5 years of sales and growth expanded abroad to new markets such as Korea, Thailand and Singapore.

3. What is NOT an example of Coca-Cola Japan's innovative success?
  (A) They invented hot and cold vending machines.
  (B) They acquired the I LOHAS water company.
  (C) They developed cashless payment systems.
  (D) They created vending machines that are good for the environment.

4. According to the article, what is the main reason behind I LOHAS' success?
  (A) A survey
  (B) A famous actor
  (C) The product is environmentally friendly.
  (D) The product has a green cap and label.

NOTES

make a difference 変化をもたらす　in pursuit of... …を追求して　feat 業績　exploit 功績
get the credit 手柄になる　innovation 革新　market segment 市場区分　penetrate 参入する

at the forefront of... …の先頭に　cashless payment systems ICカードや携帯で購入できる自販機
green-house gas 温室効果ガス　on top of... …に加えて　to name a few いくつか例を挙げると
robust 堅調な　cutting-edge 最先端の　in line with... …に合わせて

Business Focus

● **cutting-edge marketing**　最先端のマーケティング

　　ミネラルウォーターのI LOHASでは、ものごとのはじまりを表す「いろは」と、環境保護と健康生活の推進を意味する「ロハス」の造語によるネーミングを施した。また、従来のミネラルウォーター製品のペットボトルに多く用いられていた青色ではなく、緑色を使用することで環境への配慮を表現すると同時に、容易にしぼれることで手軽にエコ活動に参加できることを連想させた。

Tasks for Global Leadership

Task 1 Discuss the Points
🎧 DL 13　💿 CD1-13

本ケースのポイントに関する次の会話を聞いて、空所を埋めなさい。

Ryo: I see the Coca-Cola Company used many innovative approaches to establish its brand identity. I didn't know that it **1**_____ a jolly Santa Claus in a red suit.

Meg: It's amazing. Also, they have been sponsoring the Olympic games since 1928. I'm sure that such sponsorship is **2**_____.

Ryo: Woodruff must be a marketing genius. His genius has brought about the globalization of Coca-Cola like no other company.

Meg: Yeah, the Coca-Cola system has been a good way to **3**_____ with foreign partners. For example, the Japan Coca-Cola system consists of several bottlers which produce and distribute products very effectively.

Ryo: Absolutely. Coca-Cola Japan has taken a leadership role in terms of **4**_____ and developing new drink products.

Meg: Talking about new products, the promotion of "I LOHAS" is one of Coca-Cola Japan's **5**_____. Just by crushing and twisting thin PET bottles, consumers that buy "I LOHAS" can feel that they have become eco-friendly.

Task 2 Write Down the Points

消費者に新しい価値を提供するために、どのような行動が取られたか、本文および上の会話を参考にして、与えられた文字に続くように空所を埋めなさい。

1. The Coca-Cola Company used many **i**_____ **a**_____ to establish its **b**_____ **i**_____.
2. They **c**_____ the **i**_____ of the jolly red Santa Claus and have been **s**_____ the Olympic Games. All these things are excellent **p**_____ for the company.
3. The **p**_____ of "I LOHAS" is one of Coca-Cola Japan's **c**_____ marketing successes. The product is easily twisted and crushed, so customers can feel that they have become **e**_____.

Case 3

Act 1　Global Marketing

Enhancing Luxury Brand Identity

日本の消費者に向けたブランド構築
シャネル株式会社、パルファン・クリスチャン・ディオール・ジャポン株式会社

Mission!　日本の消費者に向けたラグジュアリー・ブランドを構築せよ！

　日本の消費者は高級ブランドを好むと考えられている。だがブランドとして確立されるのは容易でない。シャネルは高級ブランドとして知られていたが、ごく一部の富裕層のものという認識があった。世界的に有名な香水である「No.5」も、他の多くの輸入香水とともに棚に陳列されているだけであった。クリスチャン・ディオールもまたファッションブランドとしては認知されていたが、香水や化粧品は日本の消費者から支持されているとは言えなかった。両ブランドの日本法人で指揮を取ったHanspeter Kappelerは、いかにしてブランドの認知度を上げ、日本の消費者の心をとらえるかという問いの答えを探るため、自ら現場に赴いた。

Vocabulary — Bottom-up Activity

次の英語に合う日本語を選び記号で答えなさい。

1. potential　　　　　　　（　　）　　(A) ブランドの特性
2. brand identity　　　　　（　　）　　(B) 象徴的なブランド
3. consistent creed　　　　（　　）　　(C) 可能性
4. cosmetic showcase　　　（　　）　　(D) 化粧品ケース
5. functional　　　　　　　（　　）　　(E) 機能的な
6. iconic brand　　　　　　（　　）　　(F) 一貫した主義・モットー

Listening — Scanning Activity

音声を聞いて空所を埋めなさい。

The Japanese market has the potential to be very profitable for luxury brands because Japan's percentage of the worldwide sales of luxury brands has once been as high as 30%. As a result, many famous cosmetics and fashion manufacturers have attempted to **1**_____ this market. However, there are several barriers, such as unique consumer habits and high quality expectations in this most competitive market. Therefore, it is essential for these companies to have excellent marketers who deeply understand, not only brand identity, but also the best way to attract consumers.

Since the innovation of the 'little black dress,' Coco Chanel has developed the consistent creed of making clothes that are more stylish than fashionable, in addition to being **2**_____, comfortable and simple. The company's haute couture line, which is only available at Chanel's Paris store, has helped to increase the prestige of the brand. Accordingly, Chanel has been regarded as one of the most luxurious brands in Japan. In contrast, Christian Dior's initial and more recent foray into this market was much more flamboyant. Their "flower women" design embraces a more **3**_____ and colorful brand image. As a result, they have been regarded as masters of creating shapes and silhouettes, which were called the "New Look." Nevertheless, both brands are still looking to have their fame in the fashion market transfer to the perfume and **4**_____ markets in Japan.

=== NOTES ===
haute couture オートクチュール（仕立て服）　foray 進出　flamboyant 大胆な

設問を聞いて最も適切な選択肢を選びなさい。

1. Why is the Japanese luxury brand market so profitable?
   (A) Because Chanel and Christian Dior are so successful.
   (B) Because it is a difficult market to enter.
   (C) Because much of world-wide sales are from Japan.
   (D) Because it is such a competitive market.

2. What is NOT a reason for Chanel's success in the Japanese fashion market?
   (A) Their designs are beautiful.　(B) Their clothes are colorful.
   (C) Their clothing is functional.　(D) Their clothes are enjoyable to wear.

Case 3　Enhancing Luxury Brand Identity

Reading

以下の英文を読み、質問の答えとして最も適切な選択肢を選びなさい。

Setting Up a Black Corner for Chanel

Founder, Coco Chanel's philosophy has created a strong and consistent brand identity for the company, thanks to the easy to remember brand colors: black and white. There is a myth about the reason for Chanel's color usage. It has been said that Coco's brand image was influenced by the time she spent during her youth at a convent orphanage where nuns wore black and white clothes representing purity and sincerity. Regardless of the origin of the brand colors, the company became the perfume industry's iconic brand soon after the successful launch of Chanel No.5 in 1921. Japanese consumers, however, have often regarded Western fragrances as being expensive and too strong. These factors and the lack of brand identity for Chanel in Japan's retail market translated into poor sales for the company in the beginning.

When Hanspeter Kappeler started his career as a sales representative for Chanel in Japan, he noticed that Chanel No.5 was exhibited as one of many products on the shelves at perfume retailers and concluded that the company needed to establish a brand image that was different from other brands. He realized that the brand look in a retail space was an important advertising factor. When seeking new ideas for marketing, Kappeler visited various shops, including competitors, and talked with consumers. During one of these visits he found that one company successfully used blue in all their showcases and immediately decided that Chanel's representative color for their cosmetic showcases should be black. He then approached a high-end department store in Ginza to obtain exclusive space for a special black showcase for Chanel's perfume. His request was initially rejected because there were no other showcases using such dark colors at that time, and the retailer felt that Chanel's black showcase would clash with the rest of the shops on the floor. Change came with the launch of the company's new cosmetics in 1978. By offering them exclusively to only 10 stores in the first year, the stores had to accept the black look, and they did. This had a big impact on the consumer because they saw that Chanel was different from other brands. By 1986 the number of department stores that had big black Chanel corners reached 50 stores.

1. Why didn't Japanese customers buy Chanel perfume?
   (A) They disliked the brand name.
   (B) They thought the smell was too strong.
   (C) They preferred colorful packages.
   (D) They had negative feelings about Chanel.

2. What happened as a result of Mr. Kappeler's persistence?
   (A) Chanel was able to establish a brand image.
   (B) He introduced Chanel No.5 to Japan.
   (C) He had trouble with a high-end department store.
   (D) He could create the black and white image for Chanel.

Innovative Approaches at Christian Dior Cosmetics & Perfumes

CheckLink　DL 18　CD1-18

   Kappeler left Chanel after the successful launch of their cosmetics and fashion lines. By that time, he had established the company as a luxury brand leader. He then became the president of Christian Dior Cosmetics & Perfumes Japan in 1988. At the time, Christian Dior had a top brand image owing to their colorful designs and creativity, but Dior was a "sleeping brand" which could not make use of the strength of its identity. At Dior, Kappeler enjoyed the freedom of taking more innovative approaches to expanding their customer base. One such idea he came up with was the idea of promoting a new perfume line by inserting a special page with a small packet containing the new fragrance in fashion magazines. When readers opened the packet on the page they could smell the product. The campaign successfully attracted customers and created great publicity.

   Another idea of Kappeler's was a cream that improved women's figures. He observed a Western medical company promoting a topical cream for improving bodylines and instantly realized the value of the concept. He thought Dior could sell such products much better, so he convinced the French headquarters to research the product. After four years, the company finally developed a body cream that could work on cellulite to eliminate excess fat tissue. The product was named *Svelte Body Refining Gel*.

   It took some time before *Svelte* was sold in Japan because of difficulties with the pharmaceutical affairs law that regulates cosmetics for import into Japan. Some of the body cream ingredients had not previously been used in Japan, so many extra procedures were necessitated which delayed the product's launch.

Svelte did start selling in other countries however, and it was not long before word of mouth created high expectations from consumers for *Svelte* in Japan. As a result, many Japanese visited places like Harrods in England and bought the entire cream inventory. In 1995, when *Svelte* was finally approved for launch in Japan, a lot of customers rushed to department stores to buy the product. The delayed launch had created an even bigger buzz for the product. At Isetan department store there was a line on the first day of sales that ran from the eighth floor all the way to the entrance. Thanks to Kappeler's innovation, *Svelte* produced five billion yen in sales in the first year.

3. How did Japanese consumers learn about Dior's body cream prior to initial sales in Japan in 1995?
   (A) They bought it at Isetan.
   (B) Mr. Kappeler told them.
   (C) They heard about it from abroad.
   (D) They found samples in fashion magazines.

4. Why was *Svelte*'s launch delayed in Japan?
   (A) Because of availability in department stores like Harrods
   (B) Because of friction with Japanese import laws
   (C) Because some body cream ingredients were difficult to locate in Japan.
   (D) Because Dior needed to come up with 500 million yen.

NOTES

convent orphanage 修道院の児童養育施設　　retail market 小売市場　　retailer 小売業者
competitor 競合他社　　high-end 最高級の　　clash ぶつかる、調和しない

- -

customer base 顧客ベース　　topical cream 塗り薬　　cellulite セルライト層、脂肪
fat tissue 脂肪の多い部位　　pharmaceutical affairs law 薬事法　　ingredient 成分　　inventory 在庫
buzz うわさ

Business Focus

● **word of mouth** 口コミ

クリスチャン・ディオールの「スヴェルト」は口コミによるマーケティングの成功例。「スヴェルト」は、薬事法の関係により日本ではすぐに販売できないため、イギリスの有名デパートなどで先行販売した。その結果、旅行者を中心にうわさが口コミにより広がっていった。

Tasks for Global Leadership

Task 1 Discuss the Points
本ケースのポイントに関する次の会話を聞いて、空所を埋めなさい。

Mai: I was very surprised that Chanel was not a strong brand at first in Japan. Even the famous perfume Chanel No.5 was not popular in those early days.

Bob: Yeah. It seems that Japanese customers did not **1**_____. This is why one of their managers needed to take action to improve the brand identity.

Mai: Uh-huh. He realized the importance of using the company's brand colors to bring awareness to their brand in department stores. Surprisingly though, his idea of having showcases **2**_____ was rejected at first.

Bob: Allowing only ten stores to sell Chanel cosmetics on the condition that they accept Chanel's colors was clever negotiating. I see that offering somebody a privilege, like Chanel did, is **3**_____.

Mai: The same manager also introduced an interesting strategy to solve the problem Christian Dior faced when they **4**_____ *Svelte*.

Bob: Yes. It was a good idea not to delay the launch of *Svelte* when the product was held up by red tape in Japan. The buzz created by tourists when they traveled overseas to buy the product was a great way to use the **5**_____ to increase sales.

Task 2 Write Down the Points
ブランドイメージを高めるために、どのような行動が取られたか、本文および上の会話を参考にして、与えられた文字に続くように空所を埋めなさい。

1. Kappeler used the company's **b**_____ **c**_____ to **b**_____ **a**_____ to their brand in department stores.
2. He **o**_____ a **p**_____ by **a**_____ only ten stores to sell Chanel cosmetics on the condition that they accept Chanel's colors.
3. He used the **w**_____ **o**_____ **m**_____ strategy to increase sales when Christian Dior were having trouble launching *Svelte*.

Case 4

Act 2　Business Strategies

Changing a Big Company with Management of Technology

技術経営で大企業に変革を起こす

サッポロビール株式会社

Mission!　技術経営で大企業を変革せよ！

　日本を代表するビールメーカーのサッポロビールは熾烈なシェア競争に直面していた。若者を中心に軽いアルコール飲料が好まれ、特にビールの苦みや渋みが苦手な消費者が増えたが、その原因はビールの重要な原料である麦芽にあった。当初、サッポロビールの生産技術部長は麦芽の除去を試みたが、実現は困難であった。そこで麦芽を使わない製品を思いつき研究チームを立ち上げ、苦難の末、エンドウ豆タンパクを活用したすっきりした味の製品を完成した。しかし、研究所発という異例の製品のため、本社にはその価値を説明できる者がいなかった。また、同社の伝統的な味とは違い過ぎるため製品化を反対する声もあった。営業サイドも既存のビールとは異なる原料の製品をいかに顧客にアピールするかという課題を抱えていた。

Vocabulary — Bottom-up Activity

次の英語に合う日本語を選び記号で答えなさい。

1. lighter tasting alcohol　　　（　　）　　(A) 顧客と流通業者
2. commercialize the product　（　　）　　(B) 軽い味のアルコール
3. organizational change　　　（　　）　　(C) 研究所
4. research laboratory　　　　（　　）　　(D) 組織の変革
5. bitter or astringent taste　　（　　）　　(E) 製品を商品化する
6. client and distributor　　　 （　　）　　(F) 苦みや渋み

Listening — Scanning Activity

音声を聞いて空所を埋めなさい。

Sapporo Breweries has had difficulty promoting the Sapporo brand as of late. One reason was attributed to a shift in consumer drinking ¹_____. Consumers now prefer lighter tasting alcohol. Another reason has been attributed to the conservative company's resistance to adapt to trends in consumer preferences. To help the company adapt to the ²_____ in consumer drinking preferences, an engineer examined consumer trends carefully and developed a new category of alcoholic beverage that required a lot of changes to Sapporo's traditional brewing formula. To help affect drastic organizational ³_____ within the company, the engineer got workers involved in a number of successful tasks, which not only helped to improve coworkers' attitudes, but also garnered support from directors. After much hard work, his team was able to ⁴_____ *Draft One*, a beer that attracted a lot of new customers.

=== NOTES ===
brewery 飲料   as of late 最近まで   brewing formula ビールの製造レシピ   coworker 同僚
garner 獲得する

設問を聞いて最も適切な選択肢を選びなさい。

1. Why did the Sapporo brand have difficulties?
   (A) Consumers disliked light beers.
   (B) There was a shift in consumer drinking preferences.
   (C) There was no attractive beer for consumers.
   (D) Consumers tended to drink whisky.

2. Why did the engineer achieve success?
   (A) He sold a lot of beer.
   (B) He ignored coworkers' suggestions.
   (C) He improved attitudes and got help from the directors.
   (D) He could solve many problems by himself.

Reading

以下の英文を読み、質問の答えとして最も適切な選択肢を選びなさい。

Draft One

When Sapporo Breweries' market share had shrunk to 20% in the 1980s and 13% in 2003, middle managers in the company had a strong sense of crisis about the situation. One technical manager at Sapporo's beverage research laboratory was especially concerned that the younger generation preferred a lighter tasting alcohol. These customers disliked beer because it had a bitter or astringent taste. Therefore his research group started to develop a new low-alcohol beer through a new production method that did not use malt. Although he had to leave his research team to work as a production director at the new Kyushu factory, his team continued the research and finally created a new product made from split peas named *Draft One*.

At the time, however, there was much opposition to the unusual proposal made by the research laboratory. Some senior managers questioned the possible success of such a light-tasting beer that was so very different from their existing premium and traditional beers. Nobody at headquarters could appreciate or explain the value of the product. Thus it was not easy for top executives to take a risk by introducing the unfamiliar product. Moreover the members of the sales department had no idea concerning how to persuade their clients and distributors to purchase this innovative product. Consequently, headquarters took a long time to decide whether they would commercialize the new product.

1. What was the technical manager's greatest concern?
   (A) Managers cared only about the company's market share.
   (B) The laboratory should have an innovative technology.
   (C) Young people liked lighter tasting alcohol.
   (D) He had to leave for Kyushu to be a factory manager.

2. Who thought it was difficult to take a risk?
   (A) Researchers at the laboratory   (B) Top executives
   (C) Sales department members   (D) Clients and distributors

Breakthroughs

Sapporo's indecision made the technical manager decide to take action immediately. He went to headquarters and organized meetings for the process of commercializing the new beer. As he was merely a production director of a local factory, these actions were beyond his responsibilities, but he was relentless because he did not have any doubt about the necessity of his actions, and top executives did not dare to dismiss him due to his exceptional track record.

Regarding sales procedures, he instructed the sales staff about the value and benefit of the new product. He sometimes made sales calls and explained the value of the product to buyers and distributors directly. In preparing for large-scale production, he asked headquarters to gather the production directors from all of their factories, so that he could instruct them on how to produce *Draft One* correctly because this brand-new product required complex brewing procedures and quality control.

His performance motivated other staff members, and they followed his example and took on responsibilities beyond their regular tasks. As a result, the atmosphere of the company became much more positive. In addition, the company's market share in the brewery market improved from 13.1% to 14.8%, with net sales increasing by 3% from 2003 and profit increasing by 23.6 billion yen, 1.8 times as much as the previous year. In the end, breakthroughs were acknowledged throughout Sapporo Breweries, ongoing support for the change became secured, and Sapporo's case became a great example of the management of technology.

3. Why did the engineer call all the production directors?
   (A) To clearly inform them of the value and benefit of his project
   (B) To make sure they avoid interfering with sales performance
   (C) To motivate sales staff in all the factories more easily
   (D) To instruct them on how to produce the product properly

4. What happened in the end?
   (A) Market share improved by 1.7%.
   (B) Net sales increased 1.8 times.
   (C) Profit increased by 3% from 2003.
   (D) Consumers acknowledged the breakthroughs.

NOTES

market share 市場占有率　　sense of crisis 危機感　　technical manager 技術部長　　malt 麦芽
split pea スプリットピー（乾燥したエンドウ豆）　　distributor 流通業者

---

breakthrough ブレークスルー　　indecision 優柔不断　　relentless あきらめない
track record 実績、業績　　make sales calls 売り込みの電話をかける
large-scale production 大量生産　　take on responsibilities 責任を負う　　net sales 純売上
ongoing 進行中の、継続中の　　secure 保証する　　management of technology 技術経営

Business Focus

- **Management of Technology (MOT)**　技術経営

  持続的発展のために技術イノベーションを中心に経営管理を行う戦略のこと。サッポロビールでは、これまでの商品開発は本社の文系出身者が行っていたが、今回は研究所発の技術イノベーションで経営的に成功を収めた。

- **market share / net sales / profit**　市場占有率／純売上／利益

  ビール業界は市場占有率であるシェア競争が厳しく、新製品の投入やマーケティング戦略で、純売上や利益が大きく左右される。

- **take on responsibilities beyond their regular tasks**　業務を越えた役割を果たす

  新たな技術イノベーションで開発された製品を商品化するために、決められた業務や権限を越えた行動を取ることがこのケースの成功を導いた。

Tasks for Global Leadership

Task 1 Discuss the Points

🎧 DL 25   💿 CD1-25

本ケースのポイントに関する次の会話を聞いて、空所を埋めなさい。

Ryo: From this MOT case I learned the importance of ¹_____ in big firms such as Sapporo Brewery. Their engineer played a significant role in changing the mindset of a large company that was struggling with declining sales.

Meg: Yeah. His actions were very precise, which demonstrated that he was very determined to see his company's current situation improve. As a first step, he ²_____ for the launch of a new product, *Draft One*. And at these meetings he asked top executives to approve the production of *Draft One*.

Ryo: He also promoted the products to sales staff and convinced them of the ³_____, which is very interesting because as an engineer we would expect him to be only interested in technology.

Meg: I agree. He even made sales calls to the company's buyers and distributors to make sure they understood the advantages of the new product.

Ryo: His actions proved that he would not be deterred from seeing ⁴_____ *Draft One*.

Meg: That is why he had headquarters gather together the company's production directors so that he could carefully ⁵_____ to them directly.

Task 2 Write Down the Points

業績不振に陥った大企業の姿勢に変革をもたらすために、どのような行動が取られたか、本文および上の会話を参考にして、与えられた文字に続くように空所を埋めなさい。

1. One technical manager o_____ m_____ at headquarters for the launch of a new product and a_____ t_____ e_____ t_____ a_____ the production.
2. He also p_____ the product to sales staff and c_____ them of its b_____.
3. He even made sales calls to the company's b_____ and d_____ to make sure they understood the a_____ of the new product.

Case 5

Act 2　Business Strategies

Reviving a Leading Brand

時代をリードするブランドの再生

株式会社良品計画

Mission!　企業ブランドを再建せよ！

　無印良品は 1980 年にスーパーマーケットチェーンの西友のプライベートブランドとして、「わけあって、安い」をキャッチコピーに掲げて登場した。単に値段が安いというだけでなく、厳選された素材や、流通過程の効率化に加え、パッケージのデザインなどシンプルな中にも美しさを具現化した商品群が特徴であった。それらは当時のバブル経済に溺れる消費者に素材の本質の価値を再認識させるものであった。1989 年に西友から良品計画として独立して以降、90 年代を通じて無印良品は多くの消費者に支持され、10 年間で売り上げは 4 倍以上にもなった。しかし、2001 年、同社の成長神話は崩れ、株価も 6 分の 1 に下落した。新 CEO に就任した松井はブランドの復活を誓った。

Vocabulary — Bottom-up Activity

次の英語に合う日本語を選び記号で答えなさい。

1. decorative　　　(　　)　　(A) 口コミ
2. raw material　　(　　)　　(B) 株価
3. aesthetic sense　(　　)　　(C) 素材
4. word of mouth　(　　)　　(D) 飾りの多い
5. ordinary income　(　　)　　(E) 復活させる
6. share price　　　(　　)　　(F) 美的感覚
7. revive　　　　　(　　)　　(G) 経常利益

Listening — Scanning Activity

音声を聞いて空所を埋めなさい。

　MUJI is now recognized as a leading international brand, but it was originally developed as an exclusive brand for the Seiyu supermarket chain in the early 1980s. The name MUJI is the first part of the Japanese expression *Mujirushi Ryohin*, which basically means quality goods without a brand name, or literally "Non-brand Quality Goods." In those days people were enjoying Japan's bubble economy and were willing to spend money on expensive brands with a lot of ¹_____ elements. The founders of MUJI regarded such trends as unhealthy habits of consumer spending and called for a return to simplicity in daily life.

　MUJI provides good products at reasonable prices by eliminating the waste of many retail processes. For instance, they carefully select ²_____ materials, reduce manufacturing processes, and use simply designed see-through packaging. The appeal of MUJI is the way the company utilizes an aesthetic ³_____ and quiet simplicity often found in Japanese art. Thus the company's packaging, in addition to being see-through, has been designed to make the most of natural colors and highlight the shapes of materials while minimizing environmental impact and promoting recycling. The company spends very little on advertising, but through word of ⁴_____ has achieved phenomenal success thanks to customers that support their concepts.

=== NOTES ===
exclusive brand 専用ブランド　　make the most of... …を最大限に活用する　　phenomenal 驚異的な

設問を聞いて最も適切な選択肢を選びなさい。

1. According to the founders of MUJI, how did the bubble economy negatively affect Japanese society?
   (A) Consumers were too willing to waste money on frivolous packaging.
   (B) Consumers did not care enough about quality.
   (C) Consumers became unhealthy.
   (D) Consumers regarded brands like MUJI as wasteful.

2. How is MUJI able to sell their products at a reasonable price?
   (A) They recycle other company's products on top of their own.
   (B) Their packaging is see-through for clothes only.
   (C) They have done away with wasteful manufacturing processes.
   (D) The company has a sustainable design.

Reading

以下の英文を読み、質問の答えとして最も適切な選択肢を選びなさい。

Setting up Ryohin Keikaku

In the beginning, MUJI's product line consisted of 40 items, but as their customer base increased, so did the number of products they sold. They appealed to busy urban customers by providing them with simple yet beautiful goods such as clothes, stationery, food items and kitchen appliances. The first MUJI store opened in Aoyama in 1983. Ryohin Keikaku Co., Ltd. was established in 1989 to run the MUJI business, which was separated from Seiyu, Ltd. in 1990. During 1990 to 1999, the total sales expanded 4.4 times from 24.5 billion yen to 106.69 billion yen. The ordinary income jumped up from 25 million yen to 13.37 billion yen during the same period and MUJI became the most successful retail brand of the 1990s. However, in 2001 the company suddenly suffered a huge drop in ordinary income to 5.667 billion yen and their share price sank from around 17,000 yen per share to 2,800 yen. Consequently, MUJI underwent a change in leadership.

Tadamitsu Matsui became CEO in 2001 and started to revive MUJI. He visited their shops all over Japan and talked with employees directly and discovered several problems inside and outside of the company. As a result of the company's early success and rapid transformation into a big company, sectionalism had become a problem and many employees had become arrogant about their success. In addition, many merchandisers and managers conducted business based on implicit knowledge, which was not shared with or discussed with subordinates, and the company's products were not meeting the needs of their customers, which resulted in a large amount of unsold inventory. Finally, top executives failed to lead the company with effective business strategies and this caused confusion in many stores. For example, in order to compete against new rivals such as 100 Yen Shops, Uniqlo and Nitori, MUJI changed their sales strategy and started selling items that were comparable to their rivals at similarly reduced prices. Unfortunately, these items were not what their regular customers wanted and little by little the products that had long appealed to consumers disappeared from their shelves. This resulted in dissatisfied customers who took their business elsewhere.

1. From 1990 to 1999, how much did the company's ordinary income increase?
(A) 13.345 billion yen (B) 82.19 billion yen

(C) 4.4 times   (D) 106.69 billion yen

2. Which is NOT one of the reasons for the company's financial downturn in 2001?
   (A) They failed to supply customers with products that they wanted.
   (B) Store managers were authoritarian.
   (C) The quality of their products went down.
   (D) Employees became arrogant.

Reviving the MUJI Brand

Matsui proposed "management reform project 2001" and in it outlined his strategies and resolve to improve the company's situation. In fact, he demonstrated the seriousness of his resolve by throwing away 3.8 billion yen worth of clothing that was leftover stock. This event became big news and the shock of it made all the employees realize the seriousness of the reforms. Initially he emphasized mutual communication among employees and strategically organized teams to tackle specific problems. These teams restructured useless systems, making the most use of human resources, and they saw to it that business was conducted based on explicit knowledge rather than on individual implicit knowledge. More importantly, Matsui closed down many shops that were running deficits and introduced quick decision making systems for the opening of new shops. He also improved purchasing methods and sales prediction systems. Furthermore, each shop used their floor space more efficiently and layouts became more attractive. In order to enhance product lines, MUJI enlisted the help of Yoji Yamamoto, a leading fashion designer and planner, to integrate his aesthetic sense into MUJI's corporate identity. He came up with a simple yet classy clothing line and wholesome no frills sundry items for the company. On top of this, MUJI now utilizes the Internet to solicit ideas for new products from customers by allowing them to propose innovative ideas for useful goods on MUJI's website. An example of a customer's suggestion that turned into a big hit for MUJI is "Body fitting sofas"—a sofa that conforms to fit a user's body. In 2003, the company started "World MUJI" projects by collaborating with internationally famous designers such as Jasper Morrison from Britain and Italy's Enzo Mari to produce MUJI furniture. Moreover, the company opened 'MUJI to Go' at airports. With these initiatives, MUJI's total sales became 177.532 billion yen and ordinary income was raised to 16.135 billion yen in 2012. MUJI has regained its brand power and now operates 377 shops in Japan, and their product line is comprised of over 7,000 items.

3. How did Matsui communicate to his employees that he really wanted to revive the company?
   (A) He opened new stores.
   (B) He discarded a lot of clothing.
   (C) He created explicit business operations.
   (D) He changed the layouts of stores.

4. What did NOT happen as a result of the company's reforms?
   (A) New product lines
   (B) Increased revenue
   (C) Teams of workers examined and repaired impractical systems.
   (D) A furniture line was internationally designed for export.

NOTES

kitchen appliances 台所用品　　per share 一株当たり　　transformation 変革、変化
sectionalism 縦割り主義　　merchandiser マーチャンダイザー（仕入販売係）
implicit knowledge 暗黙的知識　　subordinate 部下　　meet the needs ニーズを満たす
unsold inventory 売れ残り在庫　　comparable to… …に匹敵する

- -

management reform 経営改革　　resolve 決意　　throw away 捨てる　　leftover stock 不良在庫
mutual 相互の　　see to it 取りはからう　　explicit knowledge 明示的知識　　run a deficit 赤字を出す
sales prediction 売上予測　　enlist 得る　　integrate 統合する　　corporate identity 企業理念
sundry items 雑貨　　solicit 求める　　conform to… …に合う　　initiative 戦略
be comprised of… …から成る

Business Focus

- **implicit knowledge / explicit knowledge** 暗黙的知識／明示的知識

   個人の経験に頼っていたそれまでの経営手法を改めて、社員の持っている知識を「見える化」し、暗黙的知識から明示的知識への転換を図った。その結果、誰でも共有できる経営システムを構築し、活用することで改革を実現した。

- **World MUJI** ワールド ムジ

   世界の有名デザイナーたちが MUJI の本質を具現化する目的で開発された商品群。このため彼らの名前は商品やカタログには登場しないという、まさに「無印」の究極の戦略である。

Tasks for Global Leadership

Task 1 Discuss the Points　　DL 31　CD1-31
本ケースのポイントに関する次の会話を聞いて、空所を埋めなさい。

Mai: I love the simplicity and beauty of MUJI products, but I had no idea that they underwent restructuring before.

Bob: Mmm, yes. Though they had initially **1**_____, their transformation into a big company so quickly brought about several problems—such as sectionalism.

Mai: Not to mention, they became arrogant and hesitated to share **2**_____ with store managers. Also, to compete with rivals, they reduced the price of products, which made their products less attractive.

Bob: When the new CEO, Matsui, decided to **3**_____ the company, as a first step, he disposed of unnecessary stock to make people aware of how serious the situation at MUJI was.

Mai: Umm... He also improved communication among employees and strategically organized teams to change useless systems. Then, he utilized the Internet to **4**_____ of new products.

Bob: Yes, and to improve the brand, MUJI got help from a famous designer, Yoji Yamamoto, and they collaborated with some internationally famous designers to create World MUJI. All these **5**_____ of MUJI.

Task 2 Write Down the Points
企業ブランドを再建するために、どのような行動が取られたか、本文および上の会話を参考にして、与えられた文字に続くように空所を埋めなさい。

1. Matsui threw away **l**_____ **s**_____ to make all the employees **r**_____ the seriousness of the **r**_____.
2. He improved **c**_____ among employees and strategically **o**_____ **t**_____ to change useless systems.
3. He utilized the **I**_____ to **i**_____ customers in the **d**_____ of new products.

Case 6

Act 2 Business Strategies

Negotiating with Headquarters

アメリカ本社との交渉戦術で日本の品質管理を世界標準に

インテル株式会社

Mission!　日本の品質管理を世界標準にせよ！

　今日では世界最大の半導体メーカーとして高品質を誇るインテルも、1980年代半ばまでは製品の欠陥率が高かった。しかし、日本企業は製品の欠陥率ゼロをめざしており、部品の納入業者にも当然のごとく同様の水準を要求していた。そのような状況の中、インテルの日本法人は本社から送られてくる欠陥品に対する顧客からのクレーム処理に追われていた。品質管理の改善をアメリカの本社に要求しても、日本だけの特別な仕様は認められなかった。日本側の代表である傳田はどのように中央集権的な本社と交渉し、説得すればよいのか戦略を練っていた。

Vocabulary — Bottom-up Activity

次の英語に合う日本語を選び記号で答えなさい。

1. inferior　　　　　（　）
2. quality　　　　　（　）
3. manufacturing　（　）
4. defect　　　　　（　）
5. subsidiary　　　（　）
6. tester　　　　　（　）

(A) 検査機器
(B) 子会社
(C) 不良品、欠陥品
(D) 品質
(E) 製造
(F) 劣る

Listening — Scanning Activity

音声を聞いて空所を埋めなさい。

Intel Japan struggled with inferior quality products sent from the U.S. in the early stage of start up. By sending low ¹_____ products and failing to meet the promised delivery dates, Intel forced Japanese clients to stop manufacturing occasionally. The Japan office frequently made claims about the need for the improvement of products, but the American headquarters replied that it was natural to have defects in products and there would be no problem replacing them. They also suggested that ²_____ should have prepared for potential defects and ordered more products. Therefore, it was essential for the ³_____ to fill in this gap regarding the product reliability concepts between Americans and Japanese. Intel Japan initiated ⁴_____ in order to establish rules that would become mutually agreed upon about the reliability of the products from the U.S.

NOTES
delivery date 納期

設問を聞いて最も適切な選択肢を選びなさい。

1. What did Intel occasionally force Japanese clients to do?
   (A) To keep defects
   (B) To order more products
   (C) To stop manufacturing
   (D) To guarantee delivery dates

2. What was the problem between Intel Japan and the U.S.?
   (A) Mutual agreement
   (B) The concept of product reliability
   (C) The process for ordering products
   (D) Preparations for replacements

Reading

以下の英文を読み、質問の答えとして最も適切な選択肢を選びなさい。

Implementing Communication Strategies

Denda, who is an ex-CEO of Intel Japan, reported that headquarters did not listen to the subsidiary's claim about the need for quality improvements. This was because Intel used an international strategy to seek out global economies of scale with centralized decision making.

The Japanese subsidiary decided to implement communication strategies adapted to American low-context culture. At first, they collected data about the defective Intel products from Japanese clients over a one-year period. As the local office did not have equipment capable of testing Intel products with a high level of accuracy, they needed to analyze the clients' indirect data and propose several ways to improve the reliability of semiconductors. Subsequently, they started having monthly meetings with product managers at the head office. Unfortunately, the managers from the American fabrication sector did not believe the indirect data, so they would not admit to making mistakes.

The Japanese staff thus concluded that they needed to have their own testing equipment that could offer reliable data first-hand. As a result, they requested that they be allowed to purchase some for Japan. Regrettably, headquarters replied that they did enough product testing in the U.S. and felt that there was no need for additional testing in Japan, especially since it was believed that it would be a redundant expenditure.

1. What kind of communication strategy did the Japanese subsidiary use?
   (A) They used clients' indirect data.
   (B) They adapted to American low-context culture.
   (C) They sought global economies of scale.
   (D) They made them admit their mistakes.

2. What did the Japanese staff realize?
   (A) Americans are illogical.
   (B) How expensive the testers were.

(C) The importance of overlapping investments
(D) The necessity of having their own testers

Quality Control for the Intel Corporation

As the next step, they developed strategies that were more active. They took Japanese clients to the U.S. headquarters and let them explain directly about the reliability of Intel semiconductors being inferior to the standards of Japanese companies.

They also estimated the losses caused by receiving defective products. When customers discovered that their products were inferior, they asked for a refund or exchange from the sales staff. The staff had to spend many hours coping with problems, which resulted in missed new opportunities for sales. Therefore, Denda told his subordinates to keep daily records on how many hours they had spent dealing with these problems, so he could determine the monetary impact this had on the company. He did this by multiplying the hours spent dealing with customer claims by manpower costs per hour.

Denda then appealed to the vice president with this data, explaining that the loss caused from claim management was much higher than expected in relation to the total budget for the Japanese office. "Unless we improve this situation, the company will go bankrupt," he said. Thus, he strongly suggested that the only solution was to purchase reliable testers. He knew that by obtaining and analyzing the authentic data in Japan, they could find the defects in Intel products and improve the quality of semiconductors so that Japanese customers would be satisfied. He also insisted that the Japanese case would be a good example for future quality control for the Intel Corporation.

Eventually, Denda successfully convinced headquarters, and Intel Japan set up a Japanese headquarters with a huge warehouse in Tsukuba, Ibaraki in order to test the products that came from the U.S. Once high performance tests were introduced, the quality of all semiconductors was thoroughly investigated and every defective product claim from Japanese clients was examined promptly. This enabled the office to give feedback to the clients within a short time period. In the end, the number of defective products delivered to Japanese customers was drastically reduced.

3. What did they estimate?
   (A) The losses caused by receiving defective materials
   (B) The authentic data in Japan
   (C) The reliability of Intel semiconductors
   (D) The total budget of the Japan office

4. Why did headquarters agree with Denda?
   (A) Because Tsukuba was an ideal place.
   (B) Because Japanese clients used the testers.
   (C) Because they realized the seriousness of the problem.
   (D) Because they needed customer feedback.

NOTES

ex- 前の…　　quality improvement 品質改善　　economies of scale 規模の経済(性)、スケールメリット
centralized 中央集権型の　　decision making 意思決定　　implement 実行する
low-context culture 低コンテクスト文化　　defective 欠陥がある　　accuracy 正確性
head office 本社、本部　　fabrication sector 製造部門　　first-hand じかに、直接に
expenditure 支出

---

refund 返金、払い戻し　　monetary impact 財政上の影響　　multiply かける
manpower cost 人件費　　vice president 副社長　　in relation to… …に関して　　budget 予算
go bankrupt 倒産する　　authentic 本物の、信頼の置ける　　warehouse 倉庫　　feedback 反応、意見

Business Focus

- **global economies of scale**　グローバル規模の経済、スケールメリット
  世界規模で生産量を増大させることによってコストを下げることを指す。

- **centralized decision making**　中央集権型意思決定
  本社により意思決定が行われる中央集権型の制度で、全社的な技術水準の管理ができるだけでなく、規模の経済も実現でき、コストの削減も可能になる。

- **low-context culture**　低コンテクスト文化
  具体的な数字や明確な証拠など明示的なものを優先させる文化で、欧米人との交渉には欠かせない。反対に、暗黙の了解に依存する文化を high-context culture（高コンテクスト文化）という。

Tasks for Global Leadership

Task 1 Discuss the Points
　DL 37　　CD1-37

本ケースのポイントに関する次の会話を聞いて、空所を埋めなさい。

Ryo: I think this is a good case to learn about the way to negotiate between headquarters and subsidiaries.

Meg: Yes. The way Intel headquarters used a *1*_____ and had complete control over subsidiaries was a problem for Intel Japan when they wanted to improve the product quality of semiconductors.

Ryo: Uh-huh. Because the American headquarters did not worry about product quality, Denda needed to *2*_____ adapted to American low-context culture in order to get permission to have local testing capability in Japan. This was needed for the delivery of good products for Japanese customers.

Meg: To convince Headquarters, Denda *3*_____ all the product failure data customers had reported to Intel Japan. By using this data, Intel Japan reported back to Headquarters on how bad Intel product quality was. Unfortunately though, Intel headquarters did not believe such indirect data.

Ryo: Yeah, and as a result, Denda took their clients to Intel headquarters in America to have them explain about the reality, and he also estimated the losses Intel incurred *4*_____ from Intel U.S.A.

Meg: These were effective steps to take to make headquarters notice the seriousness of the situation. In the end, thankfully, Denda was able to convince headquarters that the only solution was to purchase reliable testers to start local testing so that Intel could *5*_____.

Task 2 Write Down the Points

日本の品質管理の標準をアメリカ本社に認めさせるために、どのような行動が取られたか、本文および上の会話を参考にして、与えられた文字に続くように空所を埋めなさい。

1. Denda needed to **i**_____ **c**_____ **s**_____ adapted to American low-context culture.
2. He took their Japanese **c**_____ to Intel headquarters in America to have them **e**_____ **d**_____ about the quality of Intel semiconductors.
3. He also **e**_____ the **l**_____ Intel incurred by receiving **d**_____ products.

Case 7

Act 2　Business Strategies

Making a Challenging Business Profitable

困難なビジネスを長期的展望で黒字化に

JR 九州高速船株式会社

Mission!　　　　　長期的戦略を立てよ！

　1987年に国鉄の分割民営化で誕生したJR九州は、鉄道だけでなく新規事業として、ジェットフォイルという高速船で福岡・釜山間を結ぶ船舶事業への参入をめざした。1991年の運航以来、国際航路の運営上の様々な規制や、ジェットフォイルの複雑な管理など多くの問題に直面した。やがて従業員の必死の努力やライバルの航空会社を狙い撃ちした戦略導入などで、2000年にようやく黒字化に成功した。だが、2002年に韓国の未来高速が同一航路に参入し、再び厳しい状況に追い込まれた。2005年にJR九州高速船のCEOに就任した丸山は、単に現状を打開するだけでなく、長期的展望に立った戦略の導入を考えていた。

Vocabulary — Bottom-up Activity

次の英語に合う日本語を選び記号で答えなさい。

1. operating deficit　　　（　　）　　（A）魅力的な代替手段
2. initial prospect　　　　（　　）　　（B）航路
3. shipping route　　　　（　　）　　（C）黒字になる
4. reap a profit　　　　　（　　）　　（D）乗客を奪う
5. attractive alternative　（　　）　　（E）赤字を生むもの
6. take passengers away　（　　）　　（F）初期の展望
7. loss-maker　　　　　　（　　）　　（G）営業損失

Listening — Scanning Activity

音声を聞いて空所を埋めなさい。

As the Japan National Railway had built up a large debt of over 27 trillion yen, the Diet of Japan decided to privatize it in 1987 and **1**_____ it into one nation-wide freight company and six Japan railways group regional companies which provide passenger services to most parts of Hokkaido, Honshu, Shikoku, and Kyushu. One of the companies in the southern part of Japan, the JR Kyushu Railway Company (JRK) was operating at a **2**_____ from the beginning. This was due to the recession of the Japanese steel industry and competition from highways and airlines. The first president of JRK, Yoshitaka Ishii, felt the need to start a new business in which the company could encourage employees to overcome the difficulties associated with working for a company that was in the red and focus instead on a **3**_____ and more positive future. To this end, Ishii's idea was to start an international jetfoil business that would operate between Kyushu and Korea. Research data predicted great success if a jetfoil **4**_____ route between Fukuoka and Pusan were to be established, so JRK started conducting business internationally in 1991.

NOTES
debt 借金、負債　Diet 国会　privatize 民営化する　due to... …のために
recession 景気後退、不況　in the red 赤字になる　jetfoil 高速旅客船

設問を聞いて最も適切な選択肢を選びなさい。

1. Why was the national railway of Japan privatized in 1987?
   (A) Because of a large debt
   (B) Because passenger services would be better.
   (C) Because of the recession of the Japanese steel industry
   (D) Because of competition from highways and airlines

2. What is NOT a reason for the initial financial troubles of JRK?
   (A) A downturn in the steel industry
   (B) A preference for flying over rail travel
   (C) A desire to travel by car or bus instead of by train
   (D) An interest in travel by jetfoil

Reading

以下の英文を読み、質問の答えとして最も適切な選択肢を選びなさい。

Jetfoil Business

JRK's jetfoils use a water-jet propulsion system powered by a gas turbine engine to travel at high speeds. The vessels, called *Beetles*, float above the sea surface due to the lifting power of the frontal and rear hydrofoils, and they can cruise in choppy seas over waves as high as 3.5 meters. The ability of *Beetles* to continue service in bad weather resulted in an anticipated service rate of 96%. This service rate, which is better than the rates for airplanes, made the company's initial prospects for success look very high, especially when the travel times between Fukuoka and Pusan were considered. *Beetles* can cruise directly to the seaside city of Pusan within three hours, which is about the same amount of total time it takes someone to travel by plane. Of course the flight time from Fukuoka to Pusan takes a little less than one hour, but it also takes another hour to travel from the airport to Pusan City, and passengers need to arrive at the airport at least one hour before their flights. Thus, by setting a reasonable fare, *Beetles* were expected to be an attractive alternative to flying.

JRK predicted that they needed a load factor of 60% to reap a profit. However, in reality jetfoil operations proved complex and it took a long time to get used to operations. Accordingly, actual service rates were at 88%, a much lower number than expected. Subsequently, *Beetles* could not take passengers away from airline companies, and the resulting load factor of 32.8% only translated to 43,000 passengers and an operating deficit. To try and remedy this budget shortfall, JRK investigated the passenger market. In 1993, the top carrier was Korean Airlines with 29.9% of market share, and second was Japan Airlines (JAL) at 25.5% with a load factor of 67%. JAL was only barely above the break-even point for this route, so JRK concluded that they needed to take 10 customers away from each JAL flight to force them to operate at a loss. As most of JAL customers were part of group tours, JRK cooperated with major travel agencies to try and capture a share of JAL's business by offering cheaper package plans for group tourists.

1. Why were *Beetles* initially expected to perform at such a high service rate?
　(A) Because they have a high load factor.
　(B) Because they can operate in storms when waves are higher than 3.5

meters.
(C) Because they are so fast.
(D) Because the hydrofoils can travel in rough seas.

2. How long does it take *Beetles* to travel from Fukuoka to Pusan?
   (A) Around three hours   (B) Between one and two hours
   (C) Less than one hour   (D) It is unpredictable.

Negotiation for Strategic Partnership CheckLink DL 42 CD1-42

The route between Pusan and Fukuoka became a loss-maker for JAL and forced them to reduce services to two flights a week in 1995. The loss caused JAL to focus on their more profitable Fukuoka to Seoul route. Eventually, almost half of JAL's ex-passengers became JRK customers. In the span of three years, JRK perfected the maintenance and operation of jetfoils to significantly improve their service rate to 96%. Ultimately, this presented the *Beetles* as a more reliable and convenient form of transportation than airplanes. By 1998, 174,000 customers were using *Beetles*, and JRK became the top market share holder. In 2001, JAL stopped flying between Pusan and Fukuoka, and JRK had four jetfoils and a customer base of 299,000 passengers.

In 2002, a Korean company called Miraejet entered the market to try and break in on JRK's monopoly. The company invested a substantial amount of money and operated three jetfoils in the beginning. As both companies used similar vessels and routes, it was difficult for customers to perceive any differences in the quality of services between the companies, so a price war ensued. JRK seemed to be winning the war with increased passengers, but the company posted a loss in 2002. In 2005, JRK set up the JR Kyushu Jet Ferry Co. (JRKF), and Yasuharu Maruyama became the CEO. Maruyama was quick to perceive that cooperating with their rival to expand both companies businesses was the best way to go, so he worked a deal in 2006 with the CEO of Miraejet to coordinate efforts. JRKF and Miraejet agreed to operate jet ferries together and promote their business to customers in their respective countries, and they decided to divide future revenues according to the ratio of each company's revenue as of fiscal 2004. The combined business was a great success, and by the end of 2011 more than 4.2 million travelers have boarded *Beetles*.

3. How was JRK able to gain top share of the market in 1998?
   (A) They doubled their fleet at that time.
   (B) They improved service rates and forced JAL to stop services between Pusan and Fukuoka.
   (C) They asked JAL to concentrate their efforts on the Fukuoka to Seoul route.
   (D) They cooperated with their rival Miraejet.

4. The word "respective" in line 22 is closest in meaning to
   (A) connective   (B) individual   (C) identical   (D) combined

---

NOTES

water-jet propulsion system ウォータージェット推進式　gas turbine ガスタービン　vessel 船舶
frontal and rear hydrofoil 船体の前後の水中翼　choppy 波の荒い　service rate サービス率
load factor 座席利用率　remedy 改善する　budget shortfall 予算不足
break-even point 損益分岐点

- -

in the span of… …の間に　ultimately 最終的に　top market share holder シェア1位
Miraejet 未来高速株式会社　monopoly 独占　substantial かなりの　ensue 結果として起きる
post a loss 損失を計上する　revenue 収益　as of… …現在　fiscal 会計年度

Business Focus

- **negotiation for strategic partnership**　戦略的パートナーシップのための交渉

　競争相手と交渉を行い、戦略的パートナーシップを構築して共栄共存を図る。JR九州高速船のケースでは、ライバル企業である韓国の未来高速と協同運航を実現した。2004年の収益の比率を基準として、以後は両者の収益の合計を分配するという取り決めにした。

- **actual service rate / load factor**　就航率／乗船率

　ジェットフォイルは、あまり天候に左右されないため、就航率が航空機より高い点を消費者に訴求した。旅客業では、損益分岐点となる乗船率を超えることが経営の目標となる。

Tasks for Global Leadership

Task 1 Discuss the Points
　DL 43　　CD1-43

本ケースのポイントに関する次の会話を聞いて、空所を埋めなさい。

Mai: It's hard to believe that a railway company started a jetfoil business and competed against airlines for customers traveling between Kyushu and Pusan, Korea.

Bob: You're right! Although the operation went poorly at first and JR Kyushu faced deficits, they were able to improve their operations and eventually **1**_____ JAL.

Mai: Yes. That's because customers viewed their jetfoils as a **2**_____ of transportation than airplanes. And as a result, they became the top carrier between Kyushu and Pusan in 1998.

Bob: Unfortunately, when a Korean competitor entered this market with a similar business model, JR Kyushu's customers couldn't easily **3**_____ between the companies, so a price war ensued.

Mai: To solve this problem, Maruyama, a new CEO for the company, took a really radical approach toward this problem—he **4**_____ their rival.

Bob: Yeah! The collaboration not only included a comprehensive revenue-sharing plan, but it also brought **5**_____ of JR Kyushu's jetfoil business in Korea.

Task 2 Write Down the Points

どのような長期的展望のもとで事業が軌道に乗っていったのか、本文および上の会話を参考にして、与えられた文字に続くように空所を埋めなさい。

1. **C**_____ viewed JR Kyushu's jetfoils as a more **r**_____ and **c**_____ form of transportation than airplanes, so JR Kyushu was able to **i**_____ its **o**_____ and take customers from airline companies.

2. Maruyama **n**_____ a **s**_____ **p**_____ with their rival to solve the **p**_____ **w**_____ **p**_____ .

3. The collaboration not only included a **c**_____ **r**_____-**s**_____ plan, but it also brought great success and better promotion of JR Kyushu's jetfoil business in Korea.

Case 8

Act 3　Localization

Becoming a Representative Corporate Citizen in China

中国人のためのブランド作りと企業活動

株式会社資生堂

Mission!　現地に合わせたビジネスをせよ！

　資生堂は1981年に中国へ進出し、北京市の要請で1983年から技術供与を行った。北京を選んだのは、中国当局との長期にわたる信頼の構築を重視したからである。1994年には合弁会社を設立し、本格的に中国での生産・販売を開始することになる。気候や水質、香りに対する嗜好も日本とは異なり、中国市場限定のブランドを立ち上げることになった。サービス精神の欠如や複雑な商習慣など改善する課題は多かったが、努力の結果、信頼されるブランドを構築することができた。だが、中国事業の推進を任された太田は、さらなる中国市場での成功には、より一層の中国人向けのブランド構築や、地域社会への浸透など様々な課題があると考えていた。

Vocabulary — Bottom-up Activity

次の英語に合う日本語を選び記号で答えなさい。

1. virtue　　　　　　　　（　　）　　　　（A）専用ブランド
2. technical assistance　（　　）　　　　（B）技術援助
3. corporate citizen　　（　　）　　　　（C）おもてなし
4. joint venture　　　　（　　）　　　　（D）共同事業
5. hospitality　　　　　（　　）　　　　（E）美徳
6. exclusive brand　　　（　　）　　　　（F）企業市民
7. stagnate　　　　　　（　　）　　　　（G）停滞する

Listening — Scanning Activity

DL 45　CD1-45

音声を聞いて空所を埋めなさい。

　Shiseido's name derives from the classic Chinese text, the "Yi Jing." It means "the virtues of the Earth." Accordingly, the company respects Eastern philosophy that originated in China as well as Western medical technology. When Shiseido entered the Chinese market in 1981, they attempted to develop trust with the Chinese government, so Shiseido provided technical ¹_____ about cosmetics to Beijing in the hopes that their efforts would eventually lead to them being viewed as a relevant corporate ²_____. In 1983, they assisted a state enterprise in Beijing with the production of cosmetics named "Hua Zi," which resulted in high sales growth. In 1991, Shiseido's initial exploits were rewarded with an invitation from the government to establish a joint ³_____ with a Chinese cosmetics company for the first time. The result was the birth of Shiseido Liyuan Cosmetics Co., Ltd. However, according to Masato Ota, the general manager of Shiseido's China Business Division, it was not easy to educate the employees about one concept of the company's corporate culture, *Omotenashi*, which represents a type of Japanese ⁴_____.

NOTES

Yi Jing『易経』　　state enterprise 国営企業　　Hua Zi「華姿」(ファーツー)
Shiseido Liyuan Cosmetics Co., Ltd. 資生堂麗源化粧品有限公司

設問を聞いて最も適切な選択肢を選びなさい。　　CheckLink　DL 46　CD1-46

1. How did Shiseido develop a good relationship with the Chinese government?
(A) They developed trust.
(B) They incorporated Chinese philosophy into their name.
(C) They hired Masato Ota.
(D) They took advantage of the Chinese government.

2. What difficulty did Shiseido face when setting up a joint venture?
(A) Their activities were limited.
(B) They needed more technical assistance.
(C) They had trouble training employees in the Shiseido way of doing business.
(D) Their technical expertise was taken advantage of by the government.

Case 8　Becoming a Representative Corporate Citizen in China

Reading

以下の英文を読み、質問の答えとして最も適切な選択肢を選びなさい。

Prestige Brand from China

　Before Shiseido started producing a new line for China in 1994, they had spent the previous 10 years cooperating on the development of production technology. Therefore, they understood how factors such as climate and culture would affect their production. Accordingly, Shiseido realized that the climate in China could be extremely dry and cold, which tends to result in a greater amount of damaged skin. Also, China's water is very different from Japan's. The Chinese have hard water while the Japanese have soft water. On top of these factors, Shiseido's new line for the Chinese had to make allowances for different preferences in fragrances. In Japan, "citrus fragrances" are popular, but in China women prefer "watermelon fragrances."

　While considering the huge potential of the Chinese market, Shiseido had to develop an exclusive Chinese brand that made allowances for these factors. The new brand created to uniquely nurture the skin and enrich the beauty of the Chinese is called AUPRES. AUPRES is French for "standing by you" and was created in accordance with the line's "three highs" motto: "high image," "high quality" and "high service."

　Shiseido has spent years developing and redefining what constitutes acceptable service, but their sense of what high service entails was a difficult concept to convey to Chinese employees. Subsequently, the Japanese staff needed to work hard to educate the marketing staff and beauty consultants on Shiseido culture. They also trained their Chinese staff to have higher technical and service competence. Eventually the Chinese staff came to understand Shiseido's motto and were able to conduct business according to the "three highs" principles. This contributed greatly to the success of AUPRES and propelled AUPRES to recent double-digit growth. Another factor that aided in this line's success was its pricing. Owing to production in China, AUPRES is priced about 40% lower than cosmetic brands imported for Chinese consumers. Combined, these two factors led to AUPRES becoming China's number one cosmetic brand. Now Chinese consumers can obtain this brand in any one of 1,050 department stores in China.

1. What did NOT need to be considered during the development of the AUPRES cosmetic line?
   (A) The typical Chinese weather (B) The Chinese landscape
   (C) The Chinese skin makeup (D) China's water

2. How was AUPRES able to achieve double-digit growth?
   (A) The line was unique.
   (B) The Chinese staff excelled and the product was priced right.
   (C) The product was marketed according to Japanese values.
   (D) The brand could be sold in 870 department stores.

The Growth Engine for Shiseido Development in China

CheckLink DL 48 CD1-48

In China, Shiseido introduced a channel strategy for different market segments. They developed cosmetic specialty store channels with influential private stores in regions around the capitals of many provinces from 2004, where they not only sold their products at dedicated sales counters, but also provided customer services such as makeup consultations. In 2006, Shiseido launched the URARA line that was developed for cosmetic specialty stores. In order to avoid problems regarding difficulties collecting payments, Shiseido asked stores to pay in advance to receive goods. They accepted the condition and now there are more than 4,300 stores in China that sell the URARA line.

Masato Ota became a product manager in China for Shiseido in 2002, and since then has been continually improving branding in China. In 2008, when sales for the AUPRES line had become stagnated, he led renewal campaigns for AUPRES. The stagnation was due to the aging of their main customer base, so Shiseido needed to enhance its brand image toward the younger generation. Ota decided to use sales campaigns that focused on the seasons and utilized famous models and singers to promote their products. Such campaigns were very successful in Japan in the 1980s. For the sales promotion, Ota hired a popular Chinese actress, a singing duo and changed the product coloring to pink. The campaign was a big success and resulted in attracting new and younger customers to the AUPRES line.

Ota realized the need for Shiseido to contribute to the Chinese people and society more, in order to become a good corporate citizen. As a result of his convictions, he had Shiseido engage in cultural activities such as supporting the Shanghai Expo and holding an exhibition of Shiseido culture at the Shanghai Art Museum. In 2008, the company also started a 10-year tree-planting program in the city of Lanzhou in Gansu Province to protect the environment by reducing CO2 and creating job opportunities for local citizens.

3. The word "stagnated" in line 12 is closest in meaning to
   (A) vivid   (B) excited   (C) inactive   (D) robust

4. Why did Shiseido want stores to prepay for the right to sell URARA cosmetics?
   (A) They didn't want to have any trouble collecting their money.
   (B) They wanted to get new customers to buy their products.
   (C) Their customers insisted that they do business this way.
   (D) They were eager to improve the brand image of Shiseido.

NOTES

hard water 硬水（石灰質を多く含む）　soft water 軟水　make allowance for… …を考慮に入れる
nurture 育てる　in accordance with… …に従って　redefine 再定義する　entail 必要とする
competence 能力　double-digit growth 二ケタ成長

channel strategy チャネル戦略　specialty store 専門店　stagnation 停滞　conviction 説得
Lanzhou 蘭州市（中国北西部にある甘粛省の省都）　Gansu Province 甘粛省
job opportunity 雇用機会

Business Focus

● **pricing**　価格設定
　資生堂は中国専用の高級ブランドを現地生産することで値段を抑え、高価な輸入品に少し手の届かなかった高級志向の消費者を惹きつけることに成功した。

● **channel strategy for different market segments**
　　　　　　　　　　　　　　　　　異なる市場セグメントごとのチャネル戦略
　デパート専用の高級プレステージ用、契約個人化粧品店用、量販店向けミドルマス用の商品群というように、市場セグメントの販売チャネルごとに、顧客層に合ったブランドを投入するマーケティング戦略を実施している。

● **pay in advance**　代金前払い
　資金未回収のリスクを回避するため、代金の前払いを条件に契約店を開拓していった。

Tasks for Global Leadership

Task 1 Discuss the Points

DL 49　CD1-49

本ケースのポイントに関する次の会話を聞いて、空所を埋めなさい。

Ryo: I think Shiseido took a unique approach to enter the Chinese market. At first, they **1**_____ with the Chinese government by providing technical support.

Meg: Yes, indeed. They wanted to be a relevant corporate citizen from the beginning, and so, they **2**_____ for local customers.

Ryo: You mean the AUPRES line, right? That line was developed in order to nurture the skin and enrich the beauty of the Chinese.

Meg: Yes! Their success in China was linked to their training dedication. They **3**_____ the local staff in higher technical and service competence.

Ryo: Another interesting point about Shiseido's success was that Chinese stores **4**_____ to receive goods, which helped Shiseido avoid problems regarding payment collection.

Meg: But you know, AUPRES was not the perfect line for all people. Ota needed to **5**_____ the younger generation to avoid market stagnation. He did this successfully by utilizing sales campaigns which were once popular in Japan.

Task 2 Write Down the Points

現地に合わせたビジネスを成功させるために、どのような行動が取られたか、本文および上の会話を参考にして、与えられた文字に続くように空所を埋めなさい。

1. Shiseido wanted to be a relevant **c**_____ **c**_____ from the beginning, so they attempted to develop **t**_____ with the Chinese government by providing **t**_____ **s**_____.

2. They developed an **e**_____ Chinese brand for **l**_____ **c**_____ and in addition, worked hard to **i**_____ the **l**_____ **s**_____ in higher technical and service competence.

3. Chinese stores agreed to **p**_____ **i**_____ **a**_____ to receive goods, which helped Shiseido avoid problems regarding **p**_____ **c**_____.

Case 8　Becoming a Representative Corporate Citizen in China

Case 9

Act 3　Localization

Developing New Business in Emerging Markets
新興国の開拓者

株式会社東芝

Mission!　新興国市場に新規参入せよ！

　グローバル企業である東芝は、今や世界中に 590 のグループ会社を持つ。だが、どの国においても新規参入は容易ではなく、まずは現地の調査から入り、多様なカントリー・リスクを考えながらビジネスの機会を探っていく必要がある。特に新興国においては、大きな発展の可能性もあるが、インフラや法整備の不備、金融制度の未発達などの困難を乗り越えていかなければならない。家電事業部の藤巻は、フィリピン、インド、ロシア、ブラジルなどで、海外事業における新興国への切り込み隊長の役割を果たしていた。中でも、ベトナムでは会社設立を担当したが、90 年代はベトナム企業との合資しか許されず、政府系企業の代表者の強硬な姿勢に直面し、設立の交渉は危機に直面した。

Vocabulary — Bottom-up Activity

次の英語に合う日本語を選び記号で答えなさい。

1. tax incentive　　　　　　　　（　）　　(A) 未発達の社会基盤
2. emerging country　　　　　　（　）　　(B) 貿易商人
3. future investment　　　　　　（　）　　(C) 発展途上国
4. developing country　　　　　（　）　　(D) 将来の投資
5. market-orientated economy　（　）　　(E) 新興国
6. inadequate infrastructure　　（　）　　(F) 市場経済
7. trader　　　　　　　　　　　　（　）　　(G) 税制の優遇

Listening — Scanning Activity

音声を聞いて空所を埋めなさい。

Toshiba Corporation operates a global business network of more than 590 companies worldwide, with sales outside Japan reaching 55% of total ¹_____ in 2012. These kinds of numbers did not develop overnight though. It took a lot of foresight on Toshiba's part to realize that their future success would be linked to their ability to cultivate overseas markets. In 1974, Toshiba chose Singapore to be the location of a regional headquarters because of, in part, centrality and the ability of Toshiba's headquarters in Tokyo to use the regional office to limit risk exposure, but mostly because of tax ²_____. Toshiba Singapore Private Limited (TSP), contributes greatly to the development of ³_____ country businesses, and serves as the regional headquarters for starting businesses in Southeast Asia, Russia and Africa. According to Yoshihiro Fujimaki, an overseas operator who has worked at TSP, profits from all overseas operations are being saved in TSP bank accounts, so that the company can finance future investment projects in ⁴_____ countries. Previously, these funds have helped Toshiba penetrate into markets such as the Philippines, Russia, Vietnam, and Brazil.

NOTES
develop overnight 一夜にしてできる　　foresight 先見の明
cultivate overseas market 海外市場を開拓する　　centrality 重要性　　limit risk exposure リスクを抑える
Private Limited 有限会社　　overseas operation 海外業務　　bank account 銀行口座　　finance 出資する

設問を聞いて最も適切な選択肢を選びなさい。

1. What was the main reason behind the opening of a regional headquarters in Singapore?
   (A) To save money for business
   (B) To have a nice location
   (C) To limit the company's risk exposure
   (D) To focus on Southeast Asia

2. What does the company do with the money they save on taxes?
   (A) They save it.
   (B) They invest it.
   (C) They use it to help developing countries.
   (D) They send it to Toshiba's headquarters in Tokyo.

Reading

以下の英文を読み、質問の答えとして最も適切な選択肢を選びなさい。

Initial Investment in an Emerging Market, Vietnam

When Toshiba wants to begin operations in an emerging nation there are several steps that need to be completed before that can happen. Initially, they visit a prospective country to examine the risks. Specifically, they look to see what kinds of business opportunities are available to them, and more importantly, if there is public order and adequate security. In Vietnam, for example, when the government announced its intention to move from a centralized to a market-orientated economy in 1986, there were high expectations from abroad that the liberalization of the economy would be good for business.

When Fujimaki visited Vietnam in 1990, he discovered that despite the inadequate infrastructure and distribution channels, there was a lot of potential for future growth among the young hardworking population of over 80 million. Subsequently, he held a trade exhibition for Toshiba consumer products at a famous hotel in Ho Chi Minh City. For this event, he invited not only major retailers, but also important public figures such as the mayor and communist party higher-ups. The exhibition successfully attracted many people who were very impressed by the quality and technology of Toshiba's products. Shortly thereafter he decided to begin operations in Vietnam and entered into a business relationship with an overseas Chinese trader who had strong networks there. Unfortunately, doing business through a trader was not in Toshiba's best interest, in spite of the efficiency with which reliable traders can navigate through Vietnam's complex web of unwritten rules and regulations that are manipulated by national and local governments. Toshiba's Chinese trader increased the company's market share of products such as TVs, fridges and air-conditioners, but did so with little regard for price maintenance, and even less regard for after-sales service for consumers, which did little toward creating the kind of brand image that Toshiba desired. In the end, Fujimaki terminated the contract and set up an import agency with a government-owned electric company to help expand the business in a way that was in line with the desires of the company.

1. What is something that Toshiba is NOT concerned with when looking to begin operations in an emerging country?
   (A) The presence of crime
   (B) The business climate
   (C) The country's desire for Toshiba's products
   (D) The stability and reliability of the military

2. What is one reason why the contract with the overseas Chinese trader was terminated?
   (A) Because he was inadequate at selling Toshiba's products.
   (B) Because he became corrupt while promoting Toshiba's products.
   (C) Because he became redundant after an agent was located.
   (D) Because he cared very little for the customers after their purchase.

Toshiba Vietnam Consumer Products Co., Ltd.

CheckLink   DL 54   CD2-05

In 1993, Toshiba started the relocation of factories to Viettronics Thu Duc Company (VTD) and began expanding sales. At this time, Fujimaki decided to set up a Toshiba business office in Ho Chi Minh City at a reliable hotel that was equipped with relevant business facilities. While living and working from the hotel, he did not need to worry about security, and this approach reduced initial investment costs such as housing, renting an office and acquiring business equipment. Moreover, it would have been easy to shut down operations quickly, had it been necessary.

As a first step, the company imported TVs from Toshiba Singapore and sought to boost sales of their TVs by running advertising campaigns that featured *Oshin*. *Oshin* was a Japanese TV drama star whose portrayal of a Japanese woman's hardship won the hearts of many Vietnamese. In fact, *Oshin* was such a big hit that viewership topped more than 40% there. Toshiba had used a picture of *Oshin* with the company's logo to build brand awareness early on, but this campaign came to an abrupt end when the Ho Chi Minh City government made a policy change that forbade companies from using any non-Vietnamese language for advertisements. Fortunately for Toshiba, the government reversed this policy six months later and *Oshin* ads began running again. When domestic production of TVs began in 1998, it was the result of a joint venture between VTD and the then newly established Toshiba Vietnam Consumer Products Co., Ltd (TVCP). As there were discrepancies in the terms of the joint venture such as percentage of payout ratios, Fujimaki frequently faced difficulties in reaching a consensus agreement. However, joint ventures were the only way to do business in Vietnam and the resulting negotiations between the two companies took up a lot of time. After the success in Vietnam, Fujimaki has been involved in other overseas businesses with their most recent investment project taking place in Yangon, Myanmar when it opened up to foreign investment in 2011.

3. Why did Toshiba begin operations from a hotel room?
(A) Because the hotel was cheap and safe.
(B) Because it had a good secretary.
(C) Because it was the only place they could get permission to work from.
(D) Because it was in a good location.

4. How did Toshiba develop their brand image early on?
(A) The government helped them.
(B) They imported TVs from Singapore.
(C) They ran an effective ad campaign.
(D) They used Vietnamese in their advertising.

NOTES

business opportunity ビジネスチャンス、商機　　public order 治安
liberalization 自由化　　distribution channel 流通経路　　exhibition 見本市
consumer product 消費者製品　　public figure 著名人　　higher-up 上層部、高官
manipulate 操作する　　national government 中央政府　　local government 地方自治体
with little regard for... …を軽視して　　price maintenance 価格維持

- -

relocation of factories 生産委託　　initial investment cost 初期投資コスト　　boost 増加させる
viewership 視聴率　　brand awareness ブランドの知名度　　discrepancy 相違、食い違い
payout ratio 配当比率（利益を株主に配当する割合）　　consensus 意見の一致
foreign investment 海外投資

Business **F**ocus

● **market-orientated economy**　市場経済
　ベトナムは1986年に経済刷新政策を取り入れ、中央集権的な計画経済から資本主義的な市場経済へ移行した。

● **overseas traders**　海外貿易取引業者
　ここでは中国の華僑、インドの印僑、ユダヤ系など、世界にネットワークを持つ独立した商人たちを指す。主に金融制度が未発達な国では、代金の回収や為替リスクの肩代わりなどをする。

Tasks for Global Leadership

Task 1 Discuss the Points

DL 55   CD2-06

本ケースのポイントに関する次の会話を聞いて、空所を埋めなさい。

Mai: I've learned that it is not easy to start a business in an emerging nation. In particular, there are many risks that need to be considered when starting a business in communist countries like Vietnam.

Bob: When penetrating into Vietnam, Fujimaki **1**_____ Toshiba consumer products. This successful event was followed by Toshiba's entry into the Vietnamese market through a partnership with a Chinese trader.

Mai: It was necessary for Fujimaki to **2**_____ because traders who have established strong networks know how to deal with Vietnam's **3**_____ and regulations.

Bob: Interestingly though, Fujimaki gave up working with the trader because of the trader's lack of concern for Toshiba's brand image. This is why he **4**_____ with a government-owned electric company to help expand the business.

Mai: You definitely need to understand that it is risky **5**_____ countries.

Bob: Fortunately for Fujimaki, he could overcome a lot of setbacks and successfully develop a joint venture with a local company.

Task 2 Write Down the Points

ベトナム市場への新規参入を成功させるために、どのような行動が取られたか、本文および上の会話を参考にして、与えられた文字に続くように空所を埋めなさい。

1. Fujimaki **h**_____ a **t**_____ **e**_____ for Toshiba consumer products when **p**_____ **i**_____ Vietnam.
2. It was necessary for Fujimaki to **c**_____ with a reliable **t**_____ who had **e**_____ strong **n**_____.
3. Fujimaki **s**_____ **u**_____ an import agency with a government-owned electric company to help **e**_____ the **b**_____ and successfully developed a **j**_____ **v**_____.

Case 10

Act 3　Localization

De-centralizing Marketing Strategies

日本の消費者に伝わるコミュニケーション戦略

インテル株式会社

Mission!　　　地域の消費者と関係を築け！

　インテルの日本法人は、パソコンのCPUで9割以上のシェアを占めていたものの、アメリカの本社からはブランド力が弱いと指摘を受けていた。その理由は、市場シェアが高くても売れているのは大半が値段の安いCPUだったからである。2004年にインテルのマーケティング担当になった江田は、製品の特性や使用のメリットを伝える本社主導のそれまでのコミュニケーションのあり方に問題があると考えた。本社を説得し、日本でのブランド力を上げるために、どのようなマーケティング戦略を立案すればよいのか詳細な市場調査を行った結果、様々な問題があることが判明した。

Vocabulary — Bottom-up Activity

次の英語に合う日本語を選び記号で答えなさい。

1. multinational company　　　(　　)　　(A) 技術移転
2. centralized strategy　　　　(　　)　　(B) 明白な言葉
3. technology transfer　　　　(　　)　　(C) 親密さを構築する
4. standardized mass production　(　　)　　(D) 多国籍企業
5. explicit language　　　　　(　　)　　(E) 標準化された大量生産
6. create intimacy　　　　　　(　　)　　(F) 中央集権的な戦略

Listening — Scanning Activity

音声を聞いて空所を埋めなさい。

Intel used to operate a double marketing strategy because they needed to make and market low performance products for lower priced PCs in addition to the expansion and development of newer and more **1**_____ high performance CPUs. Unfortunately for Intel though, this sometimes led to an inverted "Performance Mix." In Japan for example, Intel CPUs hold the lion's share of the total CPU market, but their branding power was regarded as low in terms of "Performance Mix." This is because Intel headquarters evaluates the **2**_____ of a brand based on the percentage of total market share that a company's most expensive CPU holds. That is to say, Intel believes that the more expensive and high-performance CPUs a company sells, the more prestigious its brand becomes. This way of evaluating CPU brands works well in countries like the U.S., where consumers view their computers as machines and believe that the strength of a machine lies in its **3**_____ and power. Unfortunately for Intel though, Japanese consumers cared more about price than they did about performance. In fact, until recently in Japan, consumers typically bought PCs with low-performance Celeron processors in them. This led to a **4**_____ mix of 80/20. Celeron CPUs comprised 80% of the company's total sales, while their high-performance CPUs only held a 20% share.

NOTES

double marketing ダブルマーケティング（性能の高い高価な製品と、性能は高くないが値段の安い製品の2つの異なるセグメントのマーケティング）　market 市場に出す　inverted 逆転した
Performance Mix パフォーマンス・ミックス（p.60 Business Focus 参照）　lion's share 最大のシェア
Celeron セレロン（インテル社の廉価版CPU）　comprise …を占める

設問を聞いて最も適切な選択肢を選びなさい。

1. How much of the total CPU market in Japan did Intel have?
   (A) A minor share
   (B) A major share
   (C) An average share
   (D) A complete share

2. How was the Japanese CPU market different from the American market?
   (A) The Japanese cared more about specs than their counterparts.
   (B) The Americans preferred price over performance.
   (C) The Japanese were more afraid of speed than Americans.
   (D) The Americans wanted faster and more powerful PCs than the Japanese.

Reading

以下の英文を読み、質問の答えとして最も適切な選択肢を選びなさい。

Copy Exactly

Some multinational companies utilize centralized strategies to exercise control over a subsidiary's management systems and marketing—something Intel needed to do in the wake of the DRAM (Dynamic Random Access Memory) business failure. In brief, Intel, after having developed the world's first commercial memory in 1970, suffered quality control issues during mass production because local factories tended to make modifications to the DRAM, which caused lower yield rates. As a result, Intel gradually lost market share to Japanese competitors that had more advanced manufacturing processes. In 1985, they made their strategic market exit from the DRAM business and shortly thereafter introduced "copy exactly" principles so that there would not be a repeat of this incident. When Intel began specializing in the production of CPUs in 1987, they required local factories to copy the manufacturing specs they received from the U.S. exactly, to avoid the kind of technology transfer problems that had occurred previously. This resulted in local offices becoming operation centers that had to follow headquarters' standardized mass production guidelines and marketing systems.

When Makiko Eda joined Intel Japan as Marketing Director in 2004, she soon discovered problems in headquarters' "copy exactly" marketing strategies. That is, she disapproved of how explicit language was used in low-context approaches to communication to explain advanced technologies directly. Consequently, she proposed a paradigm shift to headquarters in favor of high-context approaches to communication for Japanese customers because she believed that implicit language would result in better sales for the company. Owing to Eda's background in marketing research and the results of a survey, Eda highlighted three major problems with Intel's communication strategy for the Japanese market. Her analysis revealed that; one, average people are not familiar with high technology concepts, nor do they care to understand them; two, women are not as conversant as men about Intel products; and three, business specialists, not general consumers, evaluate the value of technology. Although headquarters had initially resisted the paradigm shift, after seeing the wisdom of Eda's proposal, they agreed to let Intel Japan introduce a new high-context approach to communication.

1. What forced Intel to make a strategic exit from the DRAM market?
   (A) Centralized marketing strategies
   (B) An unacceptably low volume of sales
   (C) Copy exactly principles
   (D) Commercialization of the DRAM market

2. What did headquarters believe Intel needed to do so that they could avoid a repeat of the DRAM business failure?
   (A) Give manufactures more freedom for CPU design.
   (B) Be a little more reluctant to release new technology in the future.
   (C) Avoid standardized mass production for their overseas business.
   (D) Maintain greater control over manufacturing and marketing.

Localized Marketing Communication

   To transition to high-context approaches to communication in Japan, Eda set out to initially peak consumers' interests in the company itself. By generating greater interest in the company, she believed they could create a higher level of intimacy with consumers so that Intel would be able to better educate the Japanese on the benefits of Intel products. To this end, Intel Japan created very humorous TV commercials, which attracted a following and transformed the company into a popular brand.

   An example of one such commercial focused on a shy young boy attempting to ask a girl out. In the room was a cactus with a caption below it that read, "What if this cactus had Intel inside it?" The cactus then started shooting its thorns into the boy, with the boy repeatedly screaming "Ah, *itai* (Oh, ouch)" every time he was stung. This pun played on the Japanese phrase *aitai* (I want to see you). After hearing the phrase several times, the girl responds with, "I want to see you, too." The Japanese audience gets a good laugh at this and the commercial ends with the announcement, "Technology that evolves you, Intel."

   In addition to Intel's successful TV commercials, Eda implemented several excellent publicity campaigns that also helped improve the company's image among consumers. One time, Intel conducted a joint campaign with the Italian designer brand Furla to produce bags that businesswomen could use to carry their portable computers in. The stylish bags, limited to 500 in number, were modeled in women's fashion magazines and actively talked about on social media, which resulted in them being sold out immediately. These marketing strategies created intimacy and familiarity with general consumers in Japan and resulted in a successfully developed brand image according to the results of Nikkei BP's survey in 2007. Thanks to Eda, Intel's "Performance Mix" was improved to 50/50. She was elected President of Intel Japan in 2013 as a result of all her efforts.

3. What did Intel Japan NOT do to improve their brand image?
  (A) They created familiarity with Japanese consumers.
  (B) They created a movie about a cactus with Intel inside it.
  (C) They ran several humorous television ads.
  (D) They sold designer bags with Furla.

4. How was Eda rewarded for her all hard work?
  (A) She could collaborate with a fashion industry leader.
  (B) She was made marketing director.
  (C) She got her own TV commercial.
  (D) She became company president.

NOTES

in the wake of… …の結果として　　DRAM パソコンに使用される半導体メモリ　　yield rate 歩留まり率
manufacturing process 製造工程　　manufacturing spec 製造仕様書
low-context 低コンテクストの（p.36 Business Focus 参照）
paradigm shift パラダイム・シフト（重大な変化）　　in favor of… …を支持して
high-context 高コンテクストの　　conversant 熟知した

- -

attract a following 注目を集める　　ask out デートに誘う　　cactus サボテン
shoot thorn トゲを吹き刺す　　pun ダジャレ　　get a good laugh 爆笑する
"Technology that evolves you"「あなたを進化させるテクノロジー」
Nikkei BP's survey 日経 BP コンサルティング社が行うブランド調査

Business Focus

● **performance mix**　パフォーマンス・ミックス
　　インテルは市場でのシェアだけでなく、利益が多く出る高位機種をどれだけ高い割合で販売できるかで地域のブランド力を評価していた。この独自の評価基準を同社は「パフォーマンス・ミックス」と呼んでいる。

● **copy exactly**　完ぺきな複製
　　本社の開発した仕様や生産方式をそのまま導入することで不良品を減らし、歩留まり率を高める戦略。同様にマーケティングも本社主導型で行われていた。

Tasks for Global Leadership

Task 1 Discuss the Points   DL 61   CD2-12

本ケースのポイントに関する次の会話を聞いて、空所を埋めなさい。

Ryo: According to this case, Intel Japan held the lion's share of the total CPU market. But their branding power was regarded as low in terms of "Performance Mix" because the American headquarters *1*_____ on the percentage of total market share a company's most expensive CPU held.

Meg: When Eda became marketing manager at Intel Japan, she investigated the performance-mix dilemma and concluded that the biggest problem was the way the company used a *2*_____ in Japan based on the American context.

Ryo: You mean they used so-called *3*_____ in order to explain advanced technologies directly with explicit languages, and they used centralized communication strategies decided on by the American headquarters.

Meg: Yes, but Eda persuaded the Americans to let the Japanese office introduce high-context approaches to generate greater interest in Intel in Japan.

Ryo: She believed once a *4*_____ was created between the company and Japanese consumers, Intel would become more successful in Japan.

Meg: That's why they started showing very humorous TV commercials. I think a lot of consumers *5*_____ the company because of them.

Task 2 Write Down the Points

地域の消費者と関係を築くために、どのような行動が取られたか、本文および上の会話を参考にして、与えられた文字に続くように空所を埋めなさい。

1. The biggest problems Intel Japan had was the way they used a **c**_____ **a**_____ to consumers in Japan based on the American **c**_____.

2. Eda persuaded the Americans to let the Japanese office introduce **h**_____-**c**_____ approaches to **g**_____ greater **i**_____ in Intel in Japan.

3. Intel Japan started showing very **h**_____ TV commercials to **c**_____ **i**_____ between the company and Japanese consumers.

Case 10 De-centralizing Marketing Strategies | 61

Case 11

Act 3　Localization

Competing with Big Companies by Establishing a Regional Brand
地域密着ブランドで全国ブランドに対抗する

株式会社明月堂

Mission!　　大企業に負けない地域ブランドを確立せよ！

　明月堂がある福岡県は「饅頭・菓子王国」と呼ばれ、老舗である千鳥屋、「ひよ子」で有名な吉野堂など、資本力のある大手が存在していた。これらの企業は、早くから関東・関西の大都市に出店し、新幹線の駅にある名店街などでも販売しており、全国的に名前が通っていた。さらに、他の有力店も積極的に出店し、九州の菓子市場のシェアを奪い合っていた。このような状況において、明月堂は、これまでなかった革新的な技術で「博多通りもん」という有力商品を開発した。だが、資本力も小さく、店舗数も多くはない同社が、大手やライバルがひしめく中で、どのように販売し、売り上げを伸ばせばよいのか同社代表の秋丸は考えをめぐらしていた。

Vocabulary — Bottom-up Activity

次の英語に合う日本語を選び記号で答えなさい。

1. regional brand　　（　　）　　　　（A）日持ちする
2. confectionary　　（　　）　　　　（B）地域（地元）ブランド
3. profit margin　　（　　）　　　　（C）よく合う
4. national brand　　（　　）　　　　（D）（食品の）原料
5. ingredient　　（　　）　　　　（E）製菓
6. go well with　　（　　）　　　　（F）利益幅
7. last　　（　　）　　　　（G）全国ブランド

Listening — Scanning Activity

DL 63   CD2-14

音声を聞いて空所を埋めなさい。

The confectionary business operates in a highly competitive field in which profit ¹_____ are small. There is a commonly held belief that confectionary companies need to develop a national brand in order to generate a large volume of sales and big profits. However, Meigetsudo, which used to be a relatively small company introduced a science-based ²_____ to the confectionary business by developing a unique *manjyu* using milk and butter for *an*. The new product, *Torimon*, which retains a soft and moist texture, ³_____ for more than two weeks. This product has been awarded Gold medals by Monde Selection for many years, which has helped the firm's product become an industry leader. Unlike large companies, the firm targeted the ⁴_____ market in and around Fukuoka city to help the brand establish a strong local identity.

=== NOTES ===
commonly held belief 通念　　texture 質感
Monde Selection モンドセレクション（食品・飲料などの技術的水準を審査する民間団体）

設問を聞いて最も適切な選択肢を選びなさい。　　CheckLink   DL 64   CD2-15

1. What opinion is commonly shared between confectionary companies?
   (A) Science promotes company growth.
   (B) Moist products are important for success.
   (C) Most confectionary products last for more than two weeks.
   (D) A brand name is of critical importance.

2. Meigetsudo was initially successful because
   (A) it initially established a strong local following.
   (B) its competitors were industry giants.
   (C) it developed many different products from the beginning.
   (D) it could collaborate with the Monde Selection company.

Case 11　Competing with Big Companies by Establishing a Regional Brand

Reading

以下の英文を読み、質問の答えとして最も適切な選択肢を選びなさい。

Torimon

Market research from Meigetsudo highlighted various problems in the Japanese confectionary industry. First, the expiration date of *manjyu* is too short. Most products only last four days at most. After that period, *manjyu* lose their moisture and the products become hard. The products' life cycles are so short that firms suffer losses by having to throw away unsold *manjyu*. Second, due to significant changes in life-styles and values, the popularity of *manjyu* among the younger generation is declining because of a preference for confectionaries that contain milk and butter. Unfortunately, though, these ingredients do not traditionally go well with sweet bean or sweet potato pastes.

Despite limited financial and technical resources, Meigetsudo set two goals as a result of their market research data; one, to produce a brand new *manjyu* which would have a longer shelf-life; and two, to develop a taste that the younger generation would approve of. Akimaru, CEO of Meigetsudo, decided to employ a science-based approach to tackle the problem, so he consulted a well-known biotechnology firm that has invented many innovative ingredients, the Hayashibara Group. At the time they were contacted by Akimaru, Hayashibara had an ingredient that is made from starch called *trehalose*, which can be used as a sweetener for *an* so that the *manjyu* can last for a long period of time, but regrettably, the company did not have any products that could be used in *manjyu* to keep it soft and moist.

After two years of product research, they finally succeeded in developing the ideal *manjyu*; a baked *manjyu* that contains milk and butter and lasts for more than two weeks. The product was named *Torimon* after a local festival in Fukuoka City. After receiving positive feedback from customers, including the younger generation, Akimaru decided to promote *Torimon* as the company's flagship product.

1. What is one thing that Meigetsudo's market research did NOT highlight?
(A) *Manjyu* have been declining in popularity.
(B) *Manjyu* don't keep moist for very long.
(C) *Manjyu* have a very short shelf-life.
(D) *Manjyu* taste better when made with trehalose.

2. What was the final step Meigetsudo took before they put their new product on the market?
(A) They advertised the new product.
(B) They gave free samples out at the *Torimon* festival.
(C) They sought comments from consumers.
(D) They consulted with the Hayashibara Group.

Regional Marketing Strategies

Meigetsudo submitted *Torimon* to Monde Selection, the most famous wine and food tasting contest in the world. Their product has been awarded the Gold Medal award from 2001 to 2013 consecutively. Now, it is recognized as an excellent product and has become the standard by which all other Japanese confectionaries are judged.

In general, confectionary manufacturers are under the constant threat of being undercut by low-cost imitators, and Meigetsudo is no exception. But because the production method of *Torimon* is very complex, competitors will be hard pressed to create a reasonable facsimile of *Torimon*. Thus it can be said that this company has created a truly unique product that gives them a sustained advantage.

The CEO wanted to develop a distinguished local brand and focused on the regional market of Hakata, which is in the center of Fukuoka prefecture. Meigetsudo set up its outlets in a narrow region: in and around the Hakata area. Since their leading product *Torimon* became very popular, many companies, such as major supermarket chains and national department stores have offered to let Meigetsudo open up shops in their chains. However, Akimaru rejected these offers unless the proposed location was in and around Hakata. The CEO said, "If you can buy *Torimon* anywhere in Japan, it loses brand identity as Hakata's local heritage." According to a newspaper survey, *Torimon* became the most popular brand among visitors to Fukuoka prefecture. Accordingly, Meigetsudo has significantly increased its profit from 140 million yen in 2002 to 1.29 billion yen in 2011. This outstanding success is a very exceptional case in the Japanese confectionary industry which has been suffering from a prolonged recession in Japan and a shrinking market caused by an aging society.

3. Why is it difficult for *Torimon* to be copied?
   (A) Because the production method is very difficult.
   (B) Because it has been a Gold Medal winner for 13 years.
   (C) Because it is an excellent product.
   (D) Because imitation products are too cheap.

4. Where is *Torimon* sold?
   (A) Anywhere in Japan
   (B) In all Fukuoka department stores
   (C) In an area in the middle of Fukuoka prefecture
   (D) In supermarket chains outside of the Hakata region

NOTES

expiration date 賞味期限   moisture 湿度、水分   sweet bean 小豆など饅頭のあんに使われる豆類
paste あん   financial and technical resources 資金的・技術的資源   shelf-life 保存可能期間
Hayashibara Group 林原（でんぷんからトレハロースの製造を実現した岡山県にある技術力の高い企業）
starch でんぷん   trehalose トレハロース（甘味料）   sweetener 甘味料   flagship product 主力商品

consecutively 連続して   facsimile 複製、模写   outlet 直販店   aging society 高齢化社会

Business Focus

● **Monde Selection** モンドセレクション

1961年にヨーロッパで設立された消費生活製品の品質保証に関する審査機関。一定の水準を超えた優れた製品には金賞などの表彰が行われる。食品の評価機関としては最も権威があるため、受賞すれば商品のブランド向上に役立ちPR活動に利用できる。

● **changes in life-styles and values** ライフスタイルや価値観の変化

時代や流行と共に消費者の嗜好は変わる。ミルクやバターを入れ、しっとりとした食感を保つ焼き菓子の開発は、消費者への十分なマーケティング調査を基に実施された。

● **regional marketing strategies** 地域密着型マーケティング戦略

特定の地域でしか手に入らない希少価値の高いブランドを確立し、資源を集中させることで大企業に対抗する戦略。

Tasks for Global Leadership

Task 1 Discuss the Points
 DL 67   CD2-18

本ケースのポイントに関する次の会話を聞いて、空所を埋めなさい。

Mai: After hearing about *Torimon*, I really want to try it to learn how science has benefited the confectionary industry. You know, *Torimon* has been ¹_____ Monde Selection for many years running.

Bob: Yeah. And as a result, the firm's product became an industry leader. I still can't believe *Torimon* ²_____ for more than two weeks.

Mai: Me neither! One of the advantages of Meigetsudo's production method is that it's very complex, so competitors will be hard pressed to create a reasonable facsimile of *Torimon*.

Bob: I guess a lot of chain stores are disappointed that the CEO wouldn't sell to them because he wanted to ³_____ in Fukuoka that was available exclusively in that regional market.

Mai: You're right! But if a chain store has branches in or around Meigetsudo's regional market, and they want to sell *Torimon* in that market, they are ⁴_____.

Bob: Their CEO sure was concerned about controlling the brand identity, but I believe this strategy has been very effective at establishing an outstanding local brand. In fact, Meigetsudo has ⁵_____ as a result, which is a very rare case among confectionary companies.

Task 2 Write Down the Points
大企業に負けない地域ブランドを確立するために、どのような行動が取られたか、本文および上の会話を参考にして、与えられた文字に続くように空所を埋めなさい。

1. Meigetsudo's **p**_____ **m**_____ is very complex, so it's difficult for **c**_____ to create a reasonable facsimile of *Torimon*.
2. The CEO wouldn't sell *Torimon* to **c**_____ **s**_____ because he wanted to develop a distinguished **l**_____ **b**_____, and he also wanted it to be **a**_____ exclusively in that **r**_____ **m**_____.
3. The CEO was concerned about **c**_____ the **b**_____ **i**_____, and this strategy has been very effective at **e**_____ an outstanding local brand.

Case 12

Act 4　Globalization

Sustaining Brand Identity and Global Business Strategies

ブランド・アイデンティティの持続とグローバルビジネス戦略

株式会社良品計画

Mission!　企業文化をグローバルに展開せよ！

　今や21の国と地域で206以上の店舗を運営している良品計画も、グローバル展開においては必ずしも順調ではなかった。1991年のイギリス進出以来、11年にわたり海外でのビジネスは赤字続きであった。ヨーロッパの店舗配置の失敗、パートナー企業の離脱、中国での偽ブランドとの対峙など、様々な問題に直面した。2001年にCEOとなった松井は、経営改革の一環として、グローバル戦略の抜本的な見直しを迫られていた。

Vocabulary — Bottom-up Activity

次の英語に合う日本語を選び記号で答えなさい。

1. artful modesty　　　　　　（　　）　　　(A) 商標登録
2. cool aesthetic　　　　　　（　　）　　　(B) 賃貸料
3. currency crisis　　　　　　（　　）　　　(C) 共同経営
4. rental fee　　　　　　　　（　　）　　　(D) 無効な
5. partnership　　　　　　　（　　）　　　(E) 巧みなつつましさ
6. trademark registration　　（　　）　　　(F) クールな美学
7. invalid　　　　　　　　　（　　）　　　(G) 通貨危機

Listening — Scanning Activity

音声を聞いて空所を埋めなさい。

Today, MUJI is regarded as one of the most successful global brands among Japanese retailers. As of 2013, they were conducting business at 206 shops in 21 countries and territories. However, their overseas business initially ¹_____ several difficulties. For example, MUJI struggled to turn a profit for 11 years after opening their first overseas shop in London in 1991. This was especially disappointing considering that designers in Western countries thought the ²_____ modesty of MUJI's products was not only cool, but representative of authentic Japanese aesthetics.

Unfortunately, MUJI's products were not easily accepted as essential for daily use among consumers in Europe. Subsequently, the brand-building took much longer than expected, and with ³_____ costs very high it took time before they could make any profit in Europe. Although MUJI products had become popular in the Asia markets, such as Hong Kong, their business growth was affected by the Asian currency crisis in 1997. In 2001, Tadamitsu Matsui became CEO and hoped to quickly improve business in Europe, but struggled to develop relevant overseas business ⁴_____ by which the company could build a stronger brand and turn a stable profit internationally.

=== NOTES ===
turn a profit 利益を出す   Asian currency crisis アジア通貨危機

設問を聞いて最も適切な選択肢を選びなさい。

1. What word best describes MUJI's overseas beginnings?
   (A) Optimistic   (B) Untroubled   (C) Downbeat   (D) Stable

2. What was the consensus among Western designers about MUJI's products?
   (A) They believed MUJI would be successful.
   (B) They thought MUJI's goods were trendy.
   (C) They thought MUJI's products were high quality imitations.
   (D) They preferred Western to Japanese daily use items.

Case 12 Sustaining Brand Identity and Global Business Strategies | 69

Reading

以下の英文を読み、質問の答えとして最も適切な選択肢を選びなさい。

Business in Europe

MUJI opened their first overseas store in London in July 1991. As the company did not know how to best conduct business in the English market, they formed a partnership with Liberty Co., the U.K. company that operates the famous Liberty Department Store. Yet, as Liberty faced serious financial problems, MUJI had to quickly terminate their business relationship. This left MUJI in a difficult situation. They did not know how to rent commercial property and needed to have local agents find them appropriate locations—which resulted in higher rental fees. The fees ended up being about 20% of total revenue, which made it difficult to make a profit. When MUJI's first store in France opened in 1998, the company optimistically expected to be able to increase the number of chains to 50, but they only managed to open 23 stores in all of Europe by the end of 2003.

After becoming CEO in 2001, Matsui started reforming the company and quickly found out how critical the situation in Europe was. In 2002, both MUJI's domestic and overseas operations needed restructuring. Although MUJI in the U.K. increased sales at 16 shops, the high-cost business structures, including the exorbitant rental fees, prevented them from accumulating a surplus. In France the case was more serious in terms of being in the red, so Matsui decided to close down four shops in France as part of his management reform project.

When opening MUJI's first shop in Italy in 2004, they came up with a solution to set up a stable business. By bypassing local real-estate agents, they could find a good location at a lower rent in Milan by themselves. In addition, MUJI chose instead of the first floor, to set up shop on the second floor where cheaper rent could be had. By opening shops at "the second best location," MUJI decreased overhead by about 10% of total revenue, which enabled them to turn a profit. Hereafter, MUJI adopted to use these strategies when opening new shops.

1. What is NOT one of the problems that MUJI faced in the U.K.?
(A) Their business costs were too high.
(B) They had to terminate a business relationship.
(C) They could not find appropriate locations.
(D) They were required to go through intermediaries to rent properties.

2. What was the biggest difference between MUJI's business in Italy and the operations in the U.K. and France?

(A) Only France and the U.K. were subject to reforms.
(B) Only operations in the U.K. and France needed restructuring.
(C) Only in the U.K. and France could MUJI increase sales.
(D) Only MUJI Italy was profitable as a result of wise location choices.

Business in Asia

Just like in the U.K., MUJI formed a partnership with a famous department store group when they started doing business in Hong Kong in 1991. Their products became very popular and robust sales merited the opening of 10 stores in a relatively short time. Unfortunately, when the Asian currency crisis occurred in 1997, their partner was burdened with financial problems. As a result, MUJI could not collect their debts and had to close their business in Hong Kong. In 2001, MUJI re-entered the Hong Kong market by direct investment without any partners. They have established 10 shops in Hong Kong, which is one of the most profitable markets in the world.

MUJI attempted to enter Mainland China in 1999, but their trademark registration application was rejected because a Hong Kong-based company, JBI, had already registered "MUJI" and "Mujirushi Ryohin" in 1994. This company had imitated MUJI products and launched business in China. In 2000, Matsui filed a complaint with the Chinese patent office regarding JBI's invalid registration. It took until 2005 for Chinese officials to decide the case and during this time JBI continued selling knockoffs and expanded operations to more than 10 shops. In 2005, Matsui decided to start business in China. He began by advertising in a major Chinese newspaper, the *People's Daily* and dared to open the first official store in Shanghai in July even before JBI's registration was judged as invalid in November 2005. Nevertheless, JBI appealed the case and MUJI was kept from receiving validation until 2007. Despite these difficulties, MUJI was very successful in Shanghai and Beijing. As a result, many Chinese developers asked MUJI to open shops at their shopping malls or department stores. When opening shops, MUJI implemented a strategy similar to the one they began in Italy in 2004. They opened new shops only in places where tenant owners accepted their low-rent policy. Although this was uncommon in China, many owners agreed to the policy because the MUJI brand had name value and could attract customers to a department store or mall. In 2013, the number of shops in China reached 65.

3. How did MUJI enter the Hong Kong market the second time?
   (A) They did it on their own.
   (B) They formed a partnership.
   (C) They contracted with JBI.
   (D) They entered through Mainland China.

4. Why did tenant owners in China agree to MUJI's low-rent policy?
   (A) They knew that JBI lost the case against MUJI.
   (B) They noticed how MUJI was successful in Italy.
   (C) They heard that the owners of buildings in Hong Kong agreed to the policy.
   (D) They appreciated the brand value of MUJI.

NOTES

commercial property 商業用不動産　　exorbitant 法外な　　surplus 余り、黒字
bypass 迂回する、無視する　　real-estate agent 不動産業者　　overhead 諸経費、間接費

- -

be burdened with… …を負う　　collect one's debt 債権を回収する　　direct investment 直接投資
Mainland China 中国本土　　application 申請　　file a complaint 告訴する　　patent office 特許庁
officials 当局者　　decide a case 判決を下す　　knockoff 偽物
People's Daily 人民日報（中国共産党の機関紙）　　appeal a case 上訴する　　validation 妥当性

Business Focus

● **opening shops at "the second best location"**
　　　　　　　　　　　　　　　二等地立地展開

　良品計画は海外での成功のため、立地条件として一流商業地の１階ではなく２階など賃料の安い二等地（the second best location）を選び、固定費を抑える戦略を実施した。

● **build a stronger brand**　より強いブランドを構築する

　より強いブランドを構築することが海外での重要な成功要件である。中国では、新しい商業施設を開設する際に"MUJI"をテナントに持つことが成功条件の一つと考えられるまでになった。この結果、同社のグローバル展開の戦略の一つである家賃を抑えることも可能となった。

Tasks for Global Leadership

Task 1 Discuss the Points
 DL 73   CD2-24

本ケースのポイントに関する次の会話を聞いて、空所を埋めなさい。

Ryo: To be honest, I didn't know that MUJI was a global company, so I was surprised when I heard that their overseas business **1**_____.

Meg: The main reason for their difficulties was that their operating costs in Europe were so high that they **2**_____. And on top of this, their stores in Asia were affected by the Asian currency crisis in 1997.

Ryo: Tough breaks for MUJI. It is not easy for a company to turn a stable profit internationally, is it? Matsui's strategy to open stores in "the second best location" **3**_____ was very clever.

Meg: Their financial statements have improved very much as a result of that strategy, but fake products produced by a Hong Kong-based company proved to be quite troublesome for their overseas expansion in China.

Ryo: Yes, that was a serious issue. Court delays in China allowed the company to continue selling knockoffs, but this challenge did allow Matsui to **4**_____ to win. He opened a new store in Shanghai despite the delayed ruling in their favor.

Meg: Yeah. Eventually, MUJI established a strong brand image in China, and in addition, their overseas business has **5**_____.

Task 2 Write Down the Points

企業文化をグローバルに展開するために、どのような行動が取られたか、本文および上の会話を参考にして、与えられた文字に続くように空所を埋めなさい。

1. Matsui strategically opened stores in "the s_____ b_____ l_____" where cheaper r_____ could be had.
2. Fake products by a Hong Kong-based company caused a lot of t_____ for MUJI's o_____ e_____ in China and Matsui had to file a complaint.
3. Matsui decided to o_____ a new store in Shanghai despite the d_____, and eventually, MUJI's business began e_____ s_____ overseas.

Case 12 Sustaining Brand Identity and Global Business Strategies | 73

Case 13

Act 4　Globalization

Enhancing Global Brand Communication
グローバルブランドコミュニケーションの向上

株式会社資生堂

Mission!　グローバルブランドを確立せよ！

　資生堂は今やビジネスの半分近くを海外で行っているが、90年代半ばまでその比率は10パーセント未満であった。1872年の創業以来、美やおもてなしを追求する企業文化を持ち、化粧品ブランドとしては日本でトップの地位を確立していた。だが、化粧品の本場であるヨーロッパ進出時は無名のブランドであり、現地の商文化に合わせたマーケティングを行う必要があった。特に芸術の都であるパリでは、これまでの日本式のプロモーションはうまく機能しなかった。近年の急激なグローバル展開に伴い、重要な資産である独自の企業文化をいかに海外で理解してもらい、広めていけばよいのかが課題であった。

Vocabulary — Bottom-up Activity

CheckLink　DL 74　CD2-25

次の英語に合う日本語を選び記号で答えなさい。

1. originate　　　　　　　(　　)　　(A) 経営資源
2. package design　　　　(　　)　　(B) 由来する
3. sustain　　　　　　　　(　　)　　(C) 美容指導
4. management asset　　 (　　)　　(D) 地場の取引業者
5. local agent　　　　　　 (　　)　　(E) 維持する
6. beauty consultation　　(　　)　　(F) 容器のデザイン

Listening — Scanning Activity

音声を聞いて空所を埋めなさい。

Shiseido, Japan's first Western-style pharmacy that transformed into a cosmetics company has been operating in the Tokyo Ginza district since 1872. They set up their Design Department in 1916 and soon after became a leader in the fields of package design and 1_____ creation. In addition to their business activities, they opened the Shiseido Gallery in 1919 to help support a new generation of young artists. It was Honorary Chairman Yoshiharu Fukuhara who recognized that the strength of Shiseido's 2_____ culture was based on a long-standing tradition of respecting art. Thanks to his vision, Shiseido's overseas sales ratio of less than 10% until the mid-1990s was increased to 44.9% by 2013 as the company was transformed into a global player with operations in 89 countries and regions.

This recent accelerated 3_____ is truly remarkable considering the fact that cosmetic preferences not only differ from country to country, but are so diversely 4_____ by local cultures. Fukuhara accomplished this turnaround by redefining Shiseido's corporate culture and incorporating cultural values into business activities. In particular, he realized the importance of adapting Shiseido's distinctly Japanese cultural creed to incorporate the cultural backgrounds of whatever foreign markets they wished to expand into.

=== NOTES ===
Western-style pharmacy 西洋式の医学療法の薬を扱う薬局
Design Department 意匠部（現在の宣伝制作部）　　Honorary Chairman 名誉会長

設問を聞いて最も適切な選択肢を選びなさい。

1. Until the mid-1990s, what had been the highest overseas sales ratio ever attained by Shiseido?
   (A) More than 10%　　(B) 44.9%　　(C) Less than 10%　　(D) 89%

2. How was Chairman Fukuhara able to transform Shiseido into a global player?
   (A) He created a new package design.
   (B) He supported young artists.
   (C) He developed a new advertising campaign.
   (D) He redefined Shiseido's corporate culture.

Reading

以下の英文を読み、質問の答えとして最も適切な選択肢を選びなさい。

Number One Brand in Italy

To enter into the Italian market, Shiseido needed someone who not only understood the importance that Shiseido's corporate culture played as a significant management asset, but also knew how to articulate this asset to people inside and outside the company. One such missionary, Kunikazu Fujiwara, helped revitalize Shiseido's image in both France and Italy.

Shiseido entered the Italian market in 1963. After receiving an enthusiastic response, they accordingly opened up their first office in 1968. The company was fortunate to find capable agents who believed in the growth potential and corporate culture of Shiseido. As business gradually expanded, agents were educated in the importance of sustaining the company's creed. Fujiwara helped autonomous agents incorporate their business customs into Shiseido's unique business culture. This was a complicated task owing to the fact that cultural diversity in Italy was subject to a long history of divided politics and geography. One of the factors that contributed to Shiseido's eventual success in this market was a result of the strong connections that capable local agents made with local retailers.

Another factor that contributed to Shiseido's success was the introduction of a concept indicative of Japanese hospitality—*Omotenashi*. According to Italian business customs, some retailers reduce the prices of cosmetics considerably to increase total sales, a practice that Shiseido strongly resisted. Instead of engaging in price-cutting to increase overall sales, the company provided storefront beauty consultations to customers who bought their products. During these consultations Shiseido introduced beautification techniques to customers that were tailored to their specific skin types and tastes. By 1990, the attraction Italian customers felt for Shiseido helped the company gain the largest share of the Italian cosmetic market, which provided evidence of Shiseido's consistent effort to maximize customer satisfaction.

1. Which was NOT a factor that contributed to Shiseido's eventual success in the Italian cosmetic market?
   (A) Shiseido agents formed deep ties with local retailers.
   (B) Shiseido launched a campaign to promote the value of their products.

(C) Shiseido engaged in price-cutting.

(D) Shiseido provided advice to women on how to make themselves prettier.

2. The word "articulate" in line 3 is closest in meaning to
   (A) communicate   (B) develop   (C) create   (D) defend

Prestigious Marketing Strategies from Paris

In 1980, after a string of successes, Shiseido was ready to penetrate the French market, namely Paris, which has long been the fashion and cosmetic capital of the world. At that time, famous French artist Serge Lutens, who had been working for Christian Dior, approached Shiseido to offer his talent to support Shiseido in creating its brand in Paris. He was keen on Japanese culture and sought an opportunity to work with a company like Shiseido that possessed a hybrid culture. He proposed a ten-year plan to establish a strong brand image. At first, he presented an Eastern philosophical image by designing an impressive poster featuring a woman swimming with a red circle that evoked an image of the sun on a black lacquered background. It appealed to the French enormously by creating an authentic brand image that originated in the East. Serge consistently used the image of the sun as an important element to establish the brand. He also contributed to Shiseido's prestigious marketing strategies by his skillful use of colors in various advertising campaigns and in Shiseido's makeup and packaging designs.

When Kunikazu Fujiwara started working as a marketer in Shiseido's international division in 1990, he worked closely with Serge to help make Shiseido an even greater globally recognized brand. This transition did not happen overnight though. After struggling for five years, Fujiwara finally learned how to combine the demands of the company and customers with Serge's ability to predict color trends for cosmetics. The result was a line-up of popular new colors and designs. While working closely with the artist, Fujiwara learned how to interpret and convey Serge's revolutionary messages to other company members. This close liaison among involved parties helped facilitate the launch of Lutens' own brand Parfums-Beaute Serge Lutens in 2000. In 2007 Fujiwara became the president of Les Salons du Palais Royal Shiseido and organized global Shiseido brand communication support in 89 countries.

3. What image did Serge Lutens use the most to help establish the Shiseido brand?
  (A) A women   (B) A swimmer
  (C) An Eastern image   (D) The sun

4. What was NOT an outcome of Mr. Fujiwara and Mr. Lutens work together?
  (A) New cosmetic colors
  (B) A stronger brand image
  (C) Shiseido's hybrid culture
  (D) Mr. Luten's own line of cosmetics

NOTES

articulate 明確に述べる   missionary 伝道者   revitalize 活性化する   enthusiastic 熱狂的な
growth potential 成長性   autonomous 自律した   business custom 商習慣
cultural diversity 文化的多様性   indicative 表すもの   price-cutting 値引き   storefront 店頭の
beautification 美しくすること   tailor 合わせる

- -

a string of... 一連の…   namely すなわち   Serge Lutens セルジュ・ルタンス（1942- ）
be keen on… …に夢中になる   hybrid culture（東洋と西洋の）文化の融合
evoke 呼び起こす、連想させる   lacquered 漆を塗った   interpret 解釈する
revolutionary message 斬新な革新的メッセージ   close liaison 緊密な連携   facilitate 促進する
Parfums-Beaute Serge Lutens パルファム・セルジュ・ルタンス   Les Salons du Palais Royal
Shiseido レ・サロン・デュ・パレ・ロワイヤル・シセイドー（パリにある直営のフレグランスショップ）

Business Focus

- **prestigious marketing strategies**
  一流のクリエーター活用によるマーケティング戦略

  ヨーロッパで成功するためには、Serge Lutensのような世界一流のクリエーターを登用する必要があった。彼は1980年より資生堂の海外におけるブランドイメージの構築に貢献した。「インウイ」「資生堂メーキャップ」など多数の宣伝広告を担当した。東洋の日本発の化粧品メーカーのフランスへの浸透を、太陽を象徴する円と女性という構図を次第に変化させることで巧みに表現した。特にメーキャップの色は2年先を予言し、流行に影響を与えた。

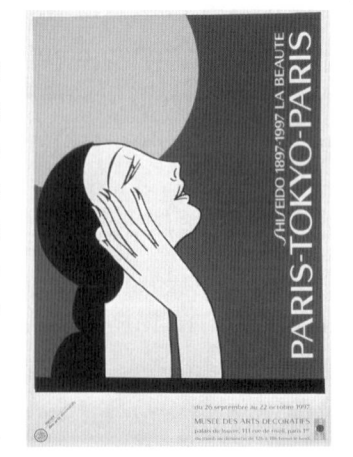

- **global brand communication**
  グローバルブランドコミュニケーション

  資生堂の海外戦略は、「Global Brand SHISEIDO」として、高級化粧品のマーケットに対応した商品にのみ「SHISEIDO」というブランド名を使用し、より付加価値の高いブランドの確立をめざしている。

Tasks for Global Leadership

Task 1 Discuss the Points

DL 79   CD2-30

本ケースのポイントに関する次の会話を聞いて、空所を埋めなさい。

Mai: It is amazing that Shiseido is the No.1 brand in Italy. This is a great feat, especially when you consider that Europe has so many strong cosmetic brands like Dior and Chanel in France for example.

Bob: I see your point. The secret of Shiseido's success comes down to the high value that they put on product design, and their 1_____ the Japanese philosophy *Omotenashi*.

Mai: So true. When entering into the Italian market, they made strong connections 2_____ who had connections with local retailers, and they provided storefront beauty consultations to customers who bought their products.

Bob: Such consistent 3_____ in Italy, but how about in France?

Mai: When starting business in France, they cooperated with the famous image creator Serge Lutens to create a brand image that highlighted Eastern aesthetics. Lutens' support in establishing their global brand not only led to many successful advertising campaigns, but Shiseido's 4_____ also improved greatly.

Bob: I heard that Shiseido success was also linked to interpreters like Fujiwara, who was great at conveying Serge's revolutionary messages to other company members. Shiseido's success proves that it takes many hard working people to 5_____.

Task 2 Write Down the Points

グローバルブランドを確立するために、どのような行動が取られたか、本文および上の会話を参考にして、与えられた文字に続くように空所を埋めなさい。

1. One of the secrets of Shiseido's success in Europe is their **c**_____ **c**_____ based on the Japanese **p**_____ *Omotenashi*.
2. In Italy, to maximize **c**_____ **s**_____ Shiseido provided storefront **b**_____ **c**_____ to customers who bought their products.
3. In France, they **c**_____ with a famous image creator to create a **b**_____ **i**_____ that highlighted Eastern aesthetics.

Case 14

Act 4　Globalization

Developing a Global Leader for Diversity Management

グローバルリーダーの育成をめざすダイバーシティ経営

株式会社東芝

TOSHIBA
Leading Innovation >>>

Mission!　グローバル人材をダイバーシティ経営で育成せよ！

　東芝は 1875 年の設立以来、日本初や世界初の様々な電気製品を開発してきた。また、早くから政府関係の製品や設備開発に関わり、家電製品だけでなく、新幹線システムや原子力発電なども手掛ける日本産業界の主流企業である。しかし、今や海外での売り上げが半分以上を占めており、外国籍の従業員も 45 パーセントに達している。これらのグローバル化に対して、伝統的な日本企業の経営理念も変化が求められるようになった。人事部門のトップとして執行役上席常務の牛尾は、いかに人材の多様化を実現し、グローバルリーダーを育成するかという明確なビジョン作りに取り組んでいた。

Vocabulary — Bottom-up Activity

次の英語に合う日本語を選び記号で答えなさい。

1. electronic product　　(　　)　　(A) 株主
2. power generator　　(　　)　　(B) 社会の基盤システム
3. direct investment　　(　　)　　(C) 発電機
4. infrastructure system　　(　　)　　(D) 電気製品
5. human resource　　(　　)　　(E) 企業理念
6. shareholder　　(　　)　　(F) 人材、人事
7. corporate philosophy　　(　　)　　(G) 直接投資

Listening — Scanning Activity

DL 81　CD2-32

音声を聞いて空所を埋めなさい。

　Toshiba's history started in 1875 when the company became Japan's first telegraph equipment manufacturer. Since then the company has developed many electrical and *1*_____ products that were firsts not only in Japan, but also the world. In Japan, for instance, they produced the first electric incandescent light bulbs, waterwheel *2*_____ generators, washing machines, and vacuum cleaners. Also, Toshiba has long been working on government-affiliated projects. During World War II, they produced power generators for the private *3*_____ and at the same time produced radios, vacuum tubes and other military supplies for the government.

　After the war, Toshiba got product licenses from American companies such as General Electric and started manufacturing and exporting their products. Thereafter the company steadily increased exports, which reached 20% of total revenues by the mid-1970s when Toshiba began to engage in direct foreign investment and set up manufacturing bases in many countries. The scope of the company's dealings has expanded to include numerous *4*_____ systems, such as railway transportation and nuclear power generation. Now the company has direct operations in more than 40 countries, with total revenues reaching 5.8 trillion yen in fiscal 2012.

=== NOTES ===
telegraph equipment 電信機　　incandescent light bulb 白熱電球
government-affiliated 政府関連の　　military supplies 軍事供給品
nuclear power generation 原子力発電

設問を聞いて最も適切な選択肢を選びなさい。　　CheckLink　DL 82　CD2-33

1. What is one of the products that Toshiba is credited with inventing?
   (A) They invented the train.
   (B) They invented the vacuum tube.
   (C) They invented a nuclear power generator.
   (D) They invented an incandescent light bulb.

2. What did Toshiba NOT produce for the government during the war?
   (A) Power generators　　(B) Vacuum tubes
   (C) Radios　　(D) Military equipment

Reading

以下の英文を読み、質問の答えとして最も適切な選択肢を選びなさい。

Globalization of Human Resources (HR)

CheckLink DL 83 CD2-34

Fumiaki Ushio, Director and head of Human Resources and Administration for Toshiba, acknowledges the necessity of diversity in management in relation to the development of globally competent business leaders. He is in charge of HR development for 206,087 employees, which is an astounding achievement considering the robust foreign influence and substantial growth the company experienced from 2004 to 2012. During these ten years, the company's foreign shareholders increased from 19% to 24.7%, while overseas sales were raised from 39.1% to 55% of total revenues, foreign subsidiaries grew from 116 to 407, and the number of employees in foreign countries multiplied from 41,000 to 93,000. Among them, there are only 1,100 Japanese workers.

Currently, the percentage of Japanese chief executives working in Toshiba's overseas subsidiaries is at 39%, with the other 61% comprised of local staff. In the near future, emerging countries are expected to yield the greatest increases, but these high-potential markets are diverse business environments with their own unique economic, political, and sociocultural systems, that will pose a challenge to Human Resources. To deal with such diversity Ushio has proposed a four-pillared approach to manage these challenges. Firstly, he believes that globalization for Toshiba must not be limited to activities outside of Japan. These changes must also be internalized in Japan. Secondly, he feels that HR must enhance the skills of Japanese staff employed abroad. Japanese workers must be adequately trained to do work effectively in foreign markets. Thirdly, he says that Toshiba's management needs to be localized. The company will need to rely on local staff to be able to operate well in foreign countries. Lastly, Ushio understands the necessity for diversity in management, and that global recruitment needs to be the norm, so that HR will have a steady pool of talented individuals to draw on at all times to fill vital positions within the company.

1. What does Fumiaki Ushio believe is essential to the development of globally competent business leaders?
    (A) The leaders must be Japanese.

(B) The leaders need special training.
(C) Efficiency in foreign markets
(D) Diversity in management

2. The word "robust" in line 5 is closest in meaning to
   (A) strong   (B) minor   (C) lively   (D) challenged

Four Pillars of Global HR for Diversity Management

Ushio's vision for global HR development includes an early selection and development system that is designed to locate and train foreign staff to contribute to the company's operations within Japan. This internal globalization is effective at developing sociocultural empathy between foreign and local Japanese staff. Namely, they come to value each other's unique religious, linguistic and cultural differences. In regard to locally adopted staff abroad, Toshiba has set up clear goals that detail how they are to be trained for top executive positions in their regions.

Toshiba's global recruitment system started in 2006. Every year, they target new graduates from top universities in foreign countries and attempt to recruit about 60 highly capable candidates who want to live and work in Japan for the long term. Their working conditions are exactly the same as Japanese employees, and they are granted permanent full-time employment with full benefits. The recruitment takes place at universities by way of seminars. Once applications from interested applicants are screened and shortlisted, the shortlisted applicants are then interviewed in their respective countries. The final candidates are invited to Japan to visit prospective working locations and have interviews. The successful candidates receive six months of intensive Japanese language training and join Toshiba's global employee programs. The new recruits are well supported and have a comprehensive training package that includes learning Japanese communication skills, business skills development, and corporate philosophy education. They also receive excellent on-the-job training by a specific supervisor who carefully monitors and supports their career progress. During the first three years of employment they are given opportunities to learn from feedback at Toshiba HR training centers. Ultimately, they are expected to become global leaders who understand Japanese corporate culture and philosophy, as well as have broader and more globally-minded worldviews.

3. According to the article, how could the training program be described?
   (A) Tender
   (B) Adequate
   (C) Satisfactory
   (D) Great

4. What is one thing that the training program for global staff does NOT include?
   (A) A personal mentor
   (B) Language training
   (C) Training at an overseas subsidiary
   (D) Training in Toshiba's ideology

NOTES

administration 管理　　competent 優秀な　　in charge of... …を任されて　　astounding 驚くべき
foreign shareholder 海外株主　　diverse 多様な　　sociocultural 社会文化的な
four-pillared 4本柱の　　internalize 内在化する　　global recruitment グローバル採用
norm 標準、基準　　draw on 活用する

- -

diversity management ダイバーシティ経営　　empathy 共感　　in regard to... …に関して
working conditions 労働条件　　permanent 永久的な　　full benefit 完全給付
by way of... …として　　applicant 応募者　　screen 選抜する　　shortlist 選考に残る
on-the-job training 研修、実地訓練　　supervisor 監督者　　globally-minded 世界志向の
worldview 世界観

Business Focus

● **diversity management**　ダイバーシティ経営

　株主、顧客、従業員、子会社など、直接経営に影響を与えるステークホルダー（利害関係者）の中で、外国人や海外への依存が高まり、その変化への対応が求められている。このような状況で、国籍や性別を問わずに優秀な人材を積極的に登用し、多様な価値観や能力を融合させて組織を活性化する「ダイバーシティ経営」の手法がグローバル時代には必要となる。

● **global recruitment**　グローバル採用

　技術系を中心に海外の優秀な学生を現地で直接採用し、日本人の新入社員と全く同じ条件で雇用して日本で勤務させながら人材を育成する制度。

Act 4　Globalization

Tasks for Global Leadership

Task 1 Discuss the Points
🎧 DL 85 💿 CD2-36

本ケースのポイントに関する次の会話を聞いて、空所を埋めなさい。

Ryo: Even a typical Japanese company like Toshiba needs to be concerned 1_____ in relation to the development of globally competent business leaders.

Meg: It's interesting, isn't it? Their future success is becoming more and more connected with overseas operations, which is why Ushio so wisely initiated 2_____ that focus on four strategies.

Ryo: He believes, first and foremost, that globalization activities should be internalized in Japan, so that all Japanese staff become more global minded.

Meg: It's a radical idea. He also expects that Japanese workers be adequately trained to 3_____.

Ryo: Another HR requirement is to have Toshiba's management localized in each country where they conduct operations. This way the company will need to 4_____ to be able to operate well in foreign countries.

Meg: Their fourth strategy is to recruit, train, and have highly capable new graduates from top universities in foreign countries come and live and work in Japan 5_____ as Japanese staff, so that these recruits might become future global leaders for the company.

Task 2 Write Down the Points

東芝の人材育成に関する４つの戦略的ガイドラインについて、本文および上の会話を参考にして、与えられた文字に続くように空所を埋めなさい。

1. **G**_____ activities should be internalized in Japan, so that all Japanese staff become more **g**_____ **m**_____.
2. Japanese workers should be adequately trained to **w**_____ **e**_____ in **f**_____ **m**_____.
3. Toshiba's **m**_____ should be **l**_____ in each country where they **c**_____ operations.
4. Toshiba should **r**_____ and **t**_____ highly **c**_____ new **g**_____ from top universities in foreign countries and have them come and live and work in Japan under the same **c**_____ as Japanese staff.

Case 14 Developing a Global Leader for Diversity Management | 85

Case 15

Act 4　Globalization

Building Global Business Models

グローバルビジネスモデルの構築

コニカミノルタ株式会社

Mission!　グローバルビジネスモデルを構築せよ！

　コニカミノルタは 2003 年にコニカとミノルタが統合して誕生した。2006 年には経営資源を集中するため、両社のかつての主力事業であったフィルムおよびカメラ事業から撤退した。同社の約 7 割の売り上げを誇る情報機器事業は、事業会社のコニカミノルタビジネステクノロジーズが担っていた。かつて同社の社長を務め、現コニカミノルタ代表執行役社長の山名は、海外大手や日本のライバル企業との競争を勝ち抜くために、いち早く構築していたドイツや東欧のビジネスネットワークや、中国での確固たる流通網を世界的な規模でうまく活用する戦略を考えていた。また将来のビジネスモデルとして、ソリューションサービス事業を推進し、高い付加価値のサービスを提供できる企業をめざしていた。このためアメリカの IT 企業を次々に買収した。だが、これらの IT サービス分野は、製造業である同社のビジネス文化にとっては新規なものであったため、適切な企業文化の融合が必要であった。

Vocabulary — Bottom-up Activity

次の英語に合う日本語を選び記号で答えなさい。

1. merger　　　　　　　　　　　　(　　)　　(A) 選択と集中
2. withdraw　　　　　　　　　　　(　　)　　(B) 駐在員事務所
3. selection and concentration　　(　　)　　(C) 製造業
4. sustainable growth　　　　　　　(　　)　　(D) 撤退する
5. representative office　　　　　　(　　)　　(E) 合併
6. manufacturing business　　　　(　　)　　(F) 持続的成長
7. multi-functional　　　　　　　　(　　)　　(G) 多機能の

Listening — Scanning Activity

音声を聞いて空所を埋めなさい。

Konica Minolta, Inc. is a Japanese technology company that was formed by a merger between Konica and Minolta in 2003. Both companies had been engaged in photo and camera businesses prior to the merger, but it was heavy losses to the tune of nine billion yen that forced Konica Minolta, Inc. to ¹_____ from both markets in 2006. The company carried out a "selection and ²_____" strategy so as to focus more on the company's manufacturing and industrial imaging product businesses. These businesses had mainly been conducted by a subsidiary, Konica Minolta Business Technologies, Inc. (KMBT), which controls about 70% of the total business. KMBT's operations revolve around MFPs (multi-functional peripherals), printers, and equipment for production print systems and graphic arts. The company also provides business ³_____ related to their business technologies business. MFPs, named "bizhubs" function as a copier, printer, scanner and fax. bizhubs can be integrated into a corporate ⁴_____ and enable a company's computers to control scanned and computer-generated data.

=== NOTES ===
to the tune of… …の額まで　　imaging product イメージング機器
revolve around …を中心に展開する
MFP コピー、プリンター、スキャナー、FAXなど多様な機能を有する複合機（multi-functional peripheralの略）　　bizhub ビズハブ（企業のITネットワークと統合することで、ビジネスのhub（拠点）になるという意味を込めた情報機器商品ブランド）　　computer-generated コンピュータで作った、CGの

設問を聞いて最も適切な選択肢を選びなさい。

1. What made Konica Minolta decide to exit the photo and camera industry?
   (A) They wanted to expand KMBT's business.
   (B) They wished to create a new subsidiary.
   (C) They wanted to be the world leader in digital color print systems.
   (D) They had suffered too many losses.

2. What function is a multi-functional peripheral unable to perform?
   (A) Scanning　　(B) Telexing　　(C) Printing　　(D) Copying

Case 15 Building Global Business Models | 87

Reading

以下の英文を読み、質問の答えとして最も適切な選択肢を選びなさい。

Global Business

Konica Minolta's digital color print systems are very famous around the world. Actually, the company is the world leader in digital color print systems. Konica Minolta's MFPs are also very popular. Their MFPs are equipped to handle many sizes of paper. In fact, Konica Minolta's MFPs are equipped to print paper as large as A3. The company's MFPs that are equipped to handle A3 sized paper have the second largest market share in America and Europe, and the top share in China.

Prior to conducting business in China, Konica Minolta started doing business in Hong Kong in the 1970s. At this time, they did not sell products in Mainland China, but their products were being distributed there through Hong Kong. At the beginning of the 1980s, Konica Minolta decided to enter the Chinese market. They became the first Japanese company in their field to set up representative offices in China. Their representative offices operated as service centers so that the company could offer maintenance to customers with Konica Minolta equipment. While they did this they were able to gradually establish service networks. These initial steps eventually led to the distribution of their products in China.

Selling products in China can be complicated. For example, when a company wants to get their products to consumers in China, they typically need to go through three kinds of distributors. The first kind of distributor is a Chinese trader who takes on the financial responsibility for collecting payments for a foreign company. These traders typically sell a foreign company's products to a second distributor. These second distributors then turn around and sell the products they received from the first distributor to a third distributor. It is the third distributor who ends up dealing directly with local shops.

1. In which market do Konica Minolta's MFPs maintain the largest share?
(A) The American market
(B) The Chinese market
(C) The European market
(D) The entire world market

2. Which is NOT mentioned as one of the roles of the Chinese distributors?
   (A) Taking on financial responsibility for collecting payments
   (B) Selling a foreign company's product to another distributor
   (C) Dealing directly with local shops
   (D) Establishing a service network

Towards Sustainable Growth

  The key to success in the Chinese market is finding as many efficient third distributors as possible. In 1990, Konica Minolta set up a joint venture with a Chinese company in Wuhan and started manufacturing there. Prior to this, they had learned about China's distribution system. Accordingly, they had made connections with relevant third distributors so as to bypass the first and second distributors. By eliminating the need to use the first and second distributors and launching into business with the third distributors directly, Konica Minolta was able to reduce costs and establish connections with the most efficient distributors. When Konica Minolta's rivals entered the Chinese market, Konica Minolta was a step ahead because of the strong networks they had developed prior to beginning manufacturing. Thanks to these connections they have been the top performer in the country since 2000.

  As you can see, Konica Minolta is a forward-thinking company. As a result, their director, Shoei Yamana is working hard to integrate more IT services into the company's business model to achieve sustainable growth. To this end, Konica Minolta strategically acquired nine American IT companies in fiscal 2011. Yamana considered these M&As essential to the future development of business innovation for Konica Minolta, but due to the different business styles of these companies, Konica Minolta needed to carefully combine these various corporate cultures together—which was not easy. Recognizing the importance of this process, Yamana requested that all the executives from Konica Minolta and the nine American IT companies be educated on each other's corporate culture.

3. What is one of the keys to success in doing business in China?
   (A) Having an office in Hong Kong
   (B) Speaking Cantonese and English
   (C) Establishing strong connections with third distributors
   (D) Setting up a joint venture

4. How was Konica Minolta able to get a jump-start on the competition in China?

(A) They had previously developed strong networks.

(B) They were prepared to risk more.

(C) They utilized strong first distributors.

(D) They educated the Chinese workers.

NOTES

go through 経由する

Wuhan 武漢（中国湖北省の省都）　　forward-thinking 前向きな、先見の明のある

M&A 企業の合併吸収（merger and acquisition の略）

Business Focus

● **selection and concentration** 選択と集中

　　グローバル競争に勝ち抜くためには、企業の中核的な技術である「コア・コンピタンス」（core competence）を中心とした、ビジネス分野の「選択と集中」が必要になってくる。

● **sustainable growth** 持続的成長

　　グローバルレベルでは、経営環境の変化は速く、あらゆる局面で多様化や複雑化が進行している。この中で、同社は持続的に成長を続けるために異分野ビジネスを融合し、変化し続ける戦略を取り入れている。

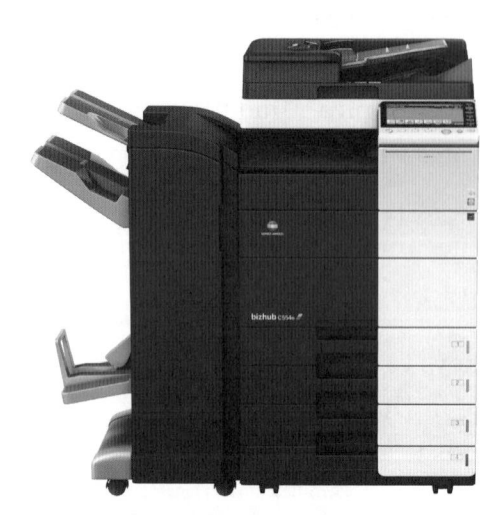

Tasks for Global Leadership

Task 1 Discuss the Points
🎧 DL 91   💿 CD2-42

本ケースのポイントに関する次の会話を聞いて、空所を埋めなさい。

Mai: According to this case, Konica Minolta is one of the world's leading companies in MFPs. Specifically, this case reports on how they ¹_____ in China.

Bob: Their initial foray into the Chinese market was very clever. They had their products distributed in China through Hong Kong prior to ²_____ in China.

Mai: Yes. And as a second step, they set up representative offices in China in the early 1980s.

Bob: This second step allowed them to ³_____ that helped them navigate China's complex distribution web.

Mai: Uh-huh. They could find ⁴_____ and save money by not having to have extra distributors.

Bob: On another note, I wonder how the integration of the recently acquired American IT companies is going. I'm sure the M&As are essential to the future development of Konica Minolta's business innovation, but the ⁵_____ companies' cultures won't be an easy task.

Task 2 Write Down the Points
グローバルビジネスモデルを構築するために、どのような行動が取られたか、本文および上の会話を参考にして、与えられた文字に続くように空所を埋めなさい。

1. Konica Minolta had their products **d**_____ in China through Hong Kong prior to starting **f**_____ **o**_____ in China.
2. They became the first Japanese company in their field to set up **r**_____ **o**_____ in China and this allowed them to establish **s**_____ **n**_____ that helped them navigate China's complex distribution web.
3. **M**_____ are essential to the future **d**_____ of Konica Minolta's business **i**_____, but the **i**_____ of newly acquired companies' cultures won't be an easy task.

謝　辞

　本書は、以下の方々の多大なるご協力を得て執筆が可能となった。お忙しい中、度重なるインタビューや講演をお願いしたが、次世代を担うグローバルリーダーの育成への協力ということで、快くとても丁寧に対応していただいた。混沌とする現代において、困難な課題をリーダーとして自ら切り開かれて、企業および地域、社会にも多大な貢献をされた方々の実話を英語のケーススタディとして形にできたのは望外の喜びである。ここに厚く感謝の意を示したい。

　なお、本書に記載した数字やデータ、及びご協力いただいた方々の肩書は2014年4月時点のものである。また、本書の内容に関する不備などは全て筆者の責任である。

　以下が、本書のケース作成にご協力いただいた方々である（掲載順）。

- インテル株式会社　元代表取締役会長
  インテル コーポレーション　元副社長
  傳田アソシエイツ株式会社　代表取締役社長
  　傳田 信行　様

- 日本コカ・コーラ株式会社　マーケティング本部副社長
  　鈴木 祥子　様

- シャネル株式会社　元セールス＆マーケティングマネージャー
  パルファン・クリスチャン・ディオール・ジャポン株式会社
  　元代表取締役社長
  ウォーターフォード・ウェッジウッド・ジャパン株式会社
  　元代表取締役社長
  KMS株式会社　代表取締役社長
  　ハンスピーター・カペラー　様

- サッポロビール株式会社　九州本部福岡支社長
  　瀬田 智則　様

- 株式会社良品計画　代表取締役会長
  　松井 忠三　様

- JR九州高速船株式会社　元代表取締役社長
  博多ターミナルビル株式会社　代表取締役社長
    丸山 康晴　様

- 株式会社資生堂　中国事業部 事業推進部部長
    太田 正人　様

- 株式会社東芝　新規開発事業部 戦略企画グループ担当部長
    藤巻 義博　様

- インテル株式会社　代表取締役社長
    江田 麻季子　様

- 株式会社 明月堂　代表取締役会長
    秋丸 卓也　様

- 株式会社資生堂　国際事業企画部次長
    レ・サロン・デュ・パレ・ロワイヤル・シセイドー　社長
    藤原 邦一　様

- 株式会社東芝　取締役　執行役上席常務
    牛尾 文昭　様

- コニカミノルタ株式会社　代表執行役社長
    山名 昌衛　様

このシールをはがすと
CheckLink 利用のための
「教科書固有番号」が
記載されています。
一度はがすと元に戻すことは
できませんのでご注意下さい。

◀ ここからはがしてください

4001
Global Leadership

本書には音声 CD（別売）があります

Global Leadership
Case Studies of Business Leaders in Japan
ビジネスケースで学ぶグローバル人材の条件

2015年1月20日　初版第1刷発行
2020年4月10日　初版第10刷発行

著者　中谷安男
　　　Ryan Smithers

発行者　福岡正人
発行所　株式会社　金星堂
（〒101-0051）東京都千代田区神田神保町 3-21
Tel. (03) 3263-3828（営業部）
　　 (03) 3263-3997（編集部）
Fax (03) 3263-0716
http://www.kinsei-do.co.jp

編集担当　今門貴浩　　　　　　　　Printed in Japan
印刷所・製本所／倉敷印刷株式会社
本書の無断複製・複写は著作権法上での例外を除き禁じられています。
本書を代行業者等の第三者に依頼してスキャンやデジタル化することは、
たとえ個人や家庭内での利用であっても認められておりません。
落丁・乱丁本はお取り替えいたします。
ISBN978-4-7647-4001-3　C1082